MARY MARY

Transparent

with Sheeri Mitchell

trueink

06 05 04 03 02   5 4 3 2 1

Library of Congress Control Number: 2002116009
ISBN: 156625-192-3

TRUEink Publishing
A division of Bonus Books
160 E. Illinois St.
Chicago, IL 60611

TABLE OF CONTENTS

A lot of people think
it's a bad thing to
grow up poor. But
how good or bad it is
depends on your
attitude more than
anything else.

The Girls

CHAPTER ONE

Tina Campbell

We wanted to run with the faster crowd sometimes. You know who they are. They're the ones that talk a little too loud, stay out a little too late and dress a little too skimpy.

Tina

Well, I guess I should start at the beginning. Erica and I were born two years apart. She was born at Saint Francis Hospital in Lynwood, California, and I, at Centinela Hospital in Inglewood, California to our parents Eddie A. and Thomasina Atkins, Jr. We were the fourth and fifth children out of nine. Yes. Nine. People always repeat that number to me as though I've made a mistake. Make no mistake. My mama gave birth to nine kids (and she looks good, too!). She and my daddy raised us all with a lot of love and laughter.

People always want to know what it was like to grow up in such a big family. Mostly it was fun. Our house was the house where everybody in the neighborhood came to hang out. My parents made sure that everybody in our neighborhood was welcome to come play or just chill. Now that I think about it, it was a smart thing for them to do. With nine children of their own, it was probably easier to keep us all in one place instead of having us all spread out over the neighborhood. My parents did a lot of smart things. The most important was teaching my siblings and me to love Jesus Christ.

In a lot of ways, my parents were more like us kids than the other grown-ups we knew. They could be silly, funny and playful. Sometimes it seemed like they were just bigger versions of us! My Mom would play hide and seek with us a lot. Can you imagine that? A grown woman hiding in the closet or behind the sofa while a six-year-old looked for her? My mom was a trip back in those days. My Dad was no different. He would let me and my sisters (after we had harassed him enough) play in and comb his hair. We'd put barrettes and bows and stuff in it. Then when he had had enough, he'd say "All right, all right! I'm not your doll!" And he'd get up with bows and barrettes all over his head. And we would laugh! As a family, we laughed a lot. I guess with nine children there's always something funny going on.

Our parents' joy was important because it made us feel safe enough to be ourselves. We never had to pretend around them. We still don't. Erica and I may be Mary Mary to the world, but we're just plain old Erica and Tina to them. If I'm having a bad day, I can literally cry on my mama's or my daddy's shoulder and get comfort. Since I'm married now (and to a very wonderful man I might add), I usually go to him. But no matter how old I get, I am still my parents' child and their shoulders are always available, too.

My parents' joy also made our home environment a loving, warm and comfortable place to grow up. I always knew that whatever drama was going on at school, in our neighborhood or with my friends, my home with my family would always be cool. Even to this day, my family is the center of my life. I could be broke, homeless, mad, whatever, but if my family is okay, then I'm straight. They're the most important thing in my life.

The word says that the joy of the Lord is our strength. And that is so true. When I was growing up, my family went through some really rough financial times. There were times when some of our cousins had to come live with us for a long time, like for eight or ten years. And sometimes we had to live with other relatives because we couldn't afford our own house to live in. Our situation was so difficult because my father developed an extremely rare and deadly physical condition called Cushing's Syndrome, a disease that affects the adrenal glands. It's a weird illness because you could be fine one week, and then for two weeks to a month find yourself bedridden with no strength or energy. The best I can describe it is that it's like the exhaustion you feel when you have the flu. Doing even the smallest things can tire you out. So when my dad was affected, he couldn't do anything but stay in bed for weeks at a time. This meant that he couldn't go to work sometimes. As the breadwinner, it was very hard on him, especially with so many mouths to feed. And I think that we kids didn't worry as much as we could have, and weren't as stressed out as we could have been because of how our parents handled these episodes.

I don't ever remember hearing my mom complain. I never heard "We don't have..." or "We can't ever..." They always gave God praise and continued to look forward to a better time. Whatever negative emotions my parents had to deal with, they never took them out on us. That's not to say that they hid things from us. We always knew what was going on in our family in as much it was our business to know. My parents didn't believe in children being able to listen to and dip in grown folks conversations. But they didn't believe in hiding things from us either. In fact it was just the opposite. They were open about our problems, prayed in faith until God changed our situation, and never stopped going to church and being faithful.

Whenever we would drive through a really nice neighborhood, my father would make sure that we understood that there was no difference between us and the people who lived in those nice homes, other than money. We weren't dumber or less important than they were. We just didn't have the finances yet. He always made sure that we knew that the finer things would be within our reach eventually. We just had to continue to love God and to obey Him and He would bless us as He saw fit.

A lot of people think it's a bad thing to grow up poor. But how good or bad it is depends on your attitude more than anything else. Since my parents were never resentful about what we didn't have, we never really focused on what we lacked. That doesn't mean we didn't complain sometimes. I was the worst. We often shopped at second hand stores for our school clothes. I hated it. In the middle of a trip, I'd say something like, "When we gon' shop at a real store? I hate wearing hand me downs!" Although it was inconvenient to be broke a lot, now that I think about it, I never really lacked anything. I never went to bed hungry. I always had clothes and a roof over my head. We didn't always have the newest video games or latest fashions. But I think that was good. We learned to be happy without those things. Our experience taught us what really mattered. We had faith and the love of each other. We'd have to be creative in our games. We'd invent toys and activities. We'd have to rely on each other for our fun, a fact that keeps us close to this day. Our parents kept teaching us that the most important things to have in our lives are God and family. I have to admit sometimes I didn't really take them very seriously; I just wanted a nice new outfit. After I got older though, I began to understand. The latest designs off of a New York runway can't make you love yourself the way God's love can. All the money in the world can't take the place of love from your sister or brother. I learned that money and stuff just made life a little easier, but they weren't life itself.

Growing up I had always known that things were tight. But I didn't really think of myself and my family as poor. Again I give credit to my parents' attitudes. They never told us that we were poor. As a matter of fact, it was just the opposite. They always made sure that we knew we were rich because we had all the things that mattered. It wasn't until I filled out the financial aid application for my first semester at El Camino Community College in Torrance, California, that I was surprised to find out that poverty level for a family of four is what my family of eleven lived on. I mean, I knew we were broke, but I didn't know that we were that broke! We weren't just poor. We was po'! It was like a bell went off in my head. How could we live as well as we did on such a little bit of money? Before I could even ask the question, I already knew the answer. Jesus Christ. The fact that my family could function on such a tiny sum of money confirmed for me what my parents always taught us. Instead of being embarrassed, I was proud and touched. For so long, through one financial struggle after the next, God took care of the Atkins family. He kept us. He never let us go homeless, hungry or unloved. He had been faithful. When I look at our situation like that, I understand my parents' joy. There they were, a housewife and husband, struggling with chronic illness, raising nine children! They had every right to be nervous wrecks, but they weren't. And let me make it clear that nobody in our house did anything illegal. There was no frauding the county, no stealing, no cheating. My parents wouldn't have stood for it. As a matter of fact, my mom tithed faithfully. Whenever money came in, God always got his ten percent off the top. They were determined that we would live the way that God wanted us to live, holy. They did their best to honor God by how they lived and he rewarded them. He kept us all.

And he didn't just keep us financially either. He kept us safe. Growing up in Inglewood, California, we were surrounded on a daily basis by all kinds of violence. Our parents made sure that we knew just because we lived in a rough area, that didn't mean that we had to be rough, too. They constantly reminded us that we were set apart for God's use. As we saw how God protected us in the midst of all the shootings and fights that went on in our city, we realized that God did have his hand on us. That's not to say that we were stuck up or thought we were better than other people. We just understood that God had plans for us (like he does for all of his children) and we wanted to follow him so we could learn what those plans were.

If Inglewood, during the time we lived there, was a war zone, then ours was a safe house. I say this because my brother, sisters and I made it through the madness that went on around us. Only my oldest brother got involved with gangs, and then he came to his senses and got out unscathed. And praise God! None of us was ever lost to gunfire. We would hear about drive-by shootings or about people's houses getting robbed, but we never experienced those things ourselves. God really kept his hand on us in that way, because there was a lot that we could have been exposed to and just weren't.

I give God credit for our protection, not because we were so good and perfect, or because somehow we earned it. Bad things happen to good people all the time. I don't know why he chose to show his love for us in that way...but I'm sure glad that he did! I give God credit, too, for making my parents so wise. Like I said above, they were a whole lot of fun. But they were also strict. God definitely used my parents' strictness to protect us. We weren't allowed to do many things or to go many places that weren't connected to family or church. Since I was a little girl, I have been a member of my uncle's church, Evangelistic Church of God in Christ. Pastor Charles Edward Lollis is his name. Pretty much everything we did was church-related: choir rehearsal, church picnics, church service. The church was our social life. We were rarely allowed to go to parties or sleepovers or things like that, especially if my parents didn't know the parents of the kids throwing the party. Now in case you get the impression that I was happy with this arrangement, let me be clear. I was not. I used to complain a lot. "We can't never do nothing fun!" was often my theme song. But it never changed my mother's mind. She understood then what many parents don't get even now. You just can't trust everybody to watch your children. Few people are going to have their backs the way you do. I mean you may trust the parents of your kids' friends, but you never know if that night at the slumber party an uncle might be over who's a little special, you know? Or if the hostess' brother is a little hot. So rather than guess, my mom just kept us close. Now don't think that we had to stay in the house all day. That wasn't the case. As a matter of fact, some of my happiest memories are of the times we went to the beach after church on Sundays. We would barbeque, swim, eat and run around. We could go places with our friends. We had freedom, but we also knew that we had a responsibility to be where we were supposed to be, when we were supposed to be there.

I mentioned that my parents were strict. They weren't overly strict, but they did believe in discipline! We had no confusion about who ran our household. Our parents spoke and we obeyed. If we didn't, they had no problem giving out a whipping (or "wuppin'" as we called them). Now let me make it very clear that my parents did not abuse us physically, mentally, emotionally or otherwise. We never had bruises, broken bones or cigarette burns. We were never spanked so hard that we couldn't walk – none of that drama. But we understood that when our parents told us to do or not to do something, they expected us to obey. The choice was always left up to us, but the consequences were left up to them. I remember my Mama used to spank us and quote scripture at the same time! "Spare the rod and spoil the child," was her favorite Proverb. She'd also say "Foolishness resides in the heart of a child, but the rod of correction will drive it out." I don't mind telling you, I hated those scriptures. And I hated the spankings, too. The funny thing is that I know that I deserved every single one that I got, and there were a lot (I was a "special" child). One of the worst offenses in our house was lying. Jesus help you if you got caught in a lie. You would get a talking to (lecture) and a spanking. I don't know which one was worse. Even though I didn't like getting spankings, like I said, I earned every one I got. If it was time to go outside, I wanted to stay in. When it was time to come in, suddenly I had to go outside. If my mother said not to touch something, I touched it. If there was prepared food set aside for a particular meal, I would sneak some and pretend to have no idea what happened to it. When it was time to go to bed, I wanted to stay up. If "no" was an answer, I argued for "yes." When "yes" was in order, I insisted on "no." If you told me something was black, I'd declare it white. I fought against going to bed, getting ready for school, eating dinner, you name it! And I had so much energy! I was always into something that I had no business even being near. I wear myself out now, just thinking about the kind of child I was. But my parents never gave up on me.

Personally, I'm glad that my parents took the time to spank me. I understand now that fear of getting a spanking helped to keep me out of a lot of trouble. There were some things that I did not even try to do, because I had the fear of my daddy in me. And I don't mean reverential awe. I mean I was just straight scared of his wrath and his belt. So whatever might stir him up, I just didn't do it. Period. Not all of my siblings required as much correction as I did. For instance, Erica was and always has been very agreeable. But I needed a lot of discipline and my parents brought it. I have observed parents who give up on disciplining their strong-willed children, because the constant correction is exhausting. To those parents I offer the encouragement of Galatians 6:9. "Do not grow weary in well doing, for you shall reap in due season if you do not faint." I don't have children yet, but I can't imagine just letting them do whatever they want without any consequences. I'm thankful that my parents were persistent when it came to discipline. I benefit from their diligence every day. As we got older, sometimes my mom might let us slide for a while, like a month or so. She'd warn you about coming home after the streetlight came on, or about running out of the house and not letting anyone know where you were, or about not doing your chores. But when she got tired of warning you, she spanked you long enough and hard enough to make up for all the times she let you slide. And by the time she was done with you, you knew exactly why she had lit into you. She was certainly fair in that way.

Another way my parents showed fairness is that they had no favorites. If one kid got a toy or a gift, then everybody else got one, too. If there wasn't enough for all of us, then nobody got anything. The closest you could say my mom got to showing favoritism is if one of us happened to catch her leaving out early on her way to the grocery store. If no one else was awake, we might have been able to convince her to let us tag along. But that was about it. Other than that, it was all for one and one for all around our house. We had a reputation for that, too. That was another way we stayed out of trouble. People in our neighborhood and school knew that if you had a beef with one Atkins, you had a beef with all of the Atkins. So if you were salty, you just shouldn't even bring it up unless you were ready to deal with all of us, cousins, too. We always put family first. Our parents taught us that. Don't get me wrong, we had our own friends, but we could not hang out with those friends if it meant that we developed an attitude with our family members because of that friendship. For example, if your friend came over and you started acting moody with your sisters just because that friend was over, then you got checked. We were to be each others' best friends first, then everyone else's.

God also worked through my dad's ministry to keep us safe. When he was growing up, my dad had the choice to lead… let's say, a less than holy life. Because of where he was raised, Merced, California, (back then a country town, full of the working poor) and the family he was born into, he could have easily given in to a criminal lifestyle. Many of his relatives did. He decided against that, but he never judged or condemned those who gave in. He ministered in prisons and in our community (even on our very block!). He befriended the young men with – ummm…less noble career aspirations – you get what I'm saying? Some people might have called them thugs or gangsters. But my dad never did. He treated them like men. He spoke to them with respect and he listened to them patiently. They confided in him and trusted him. I'm sure that for some of them, he was the only positive male role model in their lives. And because they respected him, they respected us, and our home. My dad never said to himself "Let me get to know these boys so that they don't break into my house." He had no ulterior motive. He saw a need (young men who didn't know Jesus and who had little hope or direction) and he made himself available. They loved and respected him in return. That is such a good example of what God promises. He says that if we take care of his kingdom business, he'll take care of our business. My family and I are living proof that he keeps his word.

Erica Campbell

A lot of people think it's a
bad thing to grow up poor.
But how good or bad it is
depends on your attitude more
than anything else.

Erica

It is true. Our family was spared from much of the trouble around us. As a child and as a teenager I don't think I was that aware of it though. It wasn't until I got older and was a little detached that I realized my family lived in a not-so-safe environment. When you are a child, you tend to think that everybody's life is just like yours. If you grow up in an impoverished or a violent community, you just get used to it, because that's just how life is for you. You think that the inside of your friends' houses will look like the inside of yours. You think that their parents will behave the same as yours. You assume that every city, in as much as a child is aware of cities, is just like yours. You get desensitized. Not that I think Inglewood is a horrible city. I love Inglewood, my heart and my people are in Inglewood. But where we grew up was rough. And Tina is right; we could have been pulled into a lot of different things as some of our peers were. But for the grace of God...(and the fear of our parents).

Don't get me wrong. Sometimes we were curious about the faster crowd. You know who they are. They're the ones that talk a little too loud, stay out a little too late and dress a little too skimpy. They just always seemed to be having so much fun! And we were a little curious, at least I was, just a little. But Thomasina Atkins would have none of it. Now that I'm older I can see that we didn't miss out on anything at all, except maybe getting pregnant, or getting addicted to drugs or alcohol. Our life revolved around family and church. It may sound boring, but it really wasn't. Evangelistic Church of God in Christ had and still does have a great program for young people. For us our social activities often came in the form of a choir rehearsal that lingered on so that we could talk and have fun, a party, or a picnic. I didn't think much about it then, but every moment we spent in church meant one less moment we could be in the street. I met most of my friends at church. On the occasions when I attended a party, it was usually given by somebody from church. That was good for me because it meant that all of my closest friends (most of whom were also my sisters) had relationships with Jesus just as I did. They held me accountable for living right and encouraged me to keep it up. Not to mention they would tell on me if I did anything crazy.

I don't mean to make it sound like we were perfect. We definitely weren't. Like all girls, we had our issues. But most of mine came in the form of low self-esteem. Actually Tina and I both struggled with that. The song "Little Girl" on our "Incredible" CD talks about that time in our lives. Tina has always been a handful. She freely admits that she was a "special" child. She always had so much energy. I remember that she seemed to always be getting into something. If only one person in the house was going to get in trouble, you could bet that it would be Tina. But I was more of a mellow kid. Not a saint, mind you, but just a little less energetic than my sister. Where Tina was a jokester in class, I was a more laid back student. Where she was boisterous and outspoken, I was quiet and a little reserved. She forged her own path, which often resulted in a spanking or punishment. I tended to rely on the opinions of others. Physically speaking we were different, too. She was chunky; kids made fun of her because of that. I was average height and build for my age. It's funny, even with our differences we both ended up at the same place regarding our self-esteem. Of course we handled our insecurities differently, but the cause was the same. Tina overcompensated for her poor self-image by making people laugh, whereas I wanted their approval. I guess you could say I was a
people-pleaser. The thing that's so annoying is that there was nothing really wrong with either of us. We were cute little girls. We were cute preteens and attractive teenagers. But somehow, I had gotten it into my head that I was ordinary or plain. I would look around at other little girls my age and wish that I were pretty like they were. I wanted to fit in. I wanted to be good enough. I wanted to be like everybody else. We were poor, so I was very aware that my clothes weren't fashionable. And sometimes I got teased about my clothes just as Tina got teased about her weight. Children can be really cruel. Sometimes their taunting can make you really feisty. As though you're saying "I'll show you." Or it can go the other way, making you really insecure. The criticism of my peers made me really insecure and unsure of myself. As a grown woman I now know that I had merely internalized the lies of the enemy. He's such a loser. But as a girl, I thought there was nothing really special about me at all. And I wasn't sure if I would ever do anything great. Of course that was not true at all. But back then I didn't know that.

It took until I was in my early twenties before I finally broke free of all the lies the devil had been feeding to me for years. I finally accepted myself. I said "You know what? I look like I do because this is how God made me and he did a great job!" I look like no one else because I look like Erica. I accepted that I am special, fearfully and wonderfully made in God's own image. My acceptance took in everything about me, too. I didn't just celebrate my looks, but my body, my voice, my style, my destiny. I realized that all these things were uniquely Erica and that they could never be duplicated. Having grown up in church, of course I had "known" for a long time what God's word says about me, but I finally reached the point where I was convinced that what he said about me was actually true. And that's when I changed.

I think a lot of young girls are like that. They may hear from their parents that they are beautiful and special, but they don't believe it. They may think, "You're my mother or you're my father, you have to say that." Even if they read the bible, they may think that God is not talking about them. Or they may think that the bible is not current enough to apply to their lives. All women need to hear that they are beautiful and special with a one-of-a-kind destiny. And certainly all girls do, especially from their fathers. Many girls seem to be very confident up to about sixth grade. But when they enter junior high school, their lives can fall apart. They have to put up with boys looking at them sexually. They worry about being or appearing to be "cool." They become more clothing/fashion conscious. And they really need to fit in somewhere, because junior high can be so scary for the girl who has no friends. That's why you hear so much about the violence that girls inflict on one another in school through gossip, mean-muggin', competing with and turning their backs on each other. Most of them are really insecure and would rather put up with being treated badly than to risk being alone. I think that's sad. I know that's not how God intended for us to relate to one another. I'm sure it breaks his heart. Many women carry this same mentality into adulthood, continually injuring ourselves and other women through competition, gossip and deception.

But once a girl (or woman for that matter) finally realizes her worth in Christ, she becomes really free! Once she becomes convinced that God made her beautiful and that he sees her as a gift, she has won the war. She'll be less concerned with what other people think about her, because her determination is to please God. She won't hang out with anybody who would belittle her. She'll be unafraid to go solo because she'll know God's got her back. Believing that she's valuable will prevent her from disrespecting her body. She won't engage in sex outside of marriage, abuse drugs or alcohol because she knows God's plan for her is greatness. Seeing the value in herself, she'll be able to value others. Since all of God's resources are infinite, the girl or woman who has grabbed hold of his promises knows that there's plenty to go around so why not share rather than compete?

Like the apostle Paul, I don't speak as one who has already attained perfection. I am definitely a work in progress. I have some issues with particular body parts, like my thighs. I admit they could be a bit firmer (that's more of a struggle with Haagen Dazs than anything else though). But because I embrace God's truth about me, I love me! Just as I am. I accept who I am and wouldn't want to be anyone else in the world. I am much more confident and secure than I was as a teenager and as a young adult. Because of that, I am a better friend, sister, daughter, niece, cousin, wife...woman.

Before I came to this place in my life, one struggle that grew out of my insecurity was my need to please people so that they would like me. In one way this was good. I've tried really hard to please my parents. I loved them so much; I just never wanted to make them sad. In another way, it was bad. Sometimes I was too passive. I would find myself pressured into situations that I didn't have the courage to fight against. Two examples are my first and second engagements. The first time I was engaged I was nineteen years old. He was someone I had met when I was sixteen. He was a good guy. He was in the church and he was saved. He was a little guy, but he had a big personality. He acted more like a bossy father than a boyfriend. And at some point, I concluded that I didn't want to be with him anymore. But I stayed in the relationship anyway. Then he proposed to me and I said yes! I knew that I could not possibly spend my life with him. But the reason I said yes was because he had asked and I didn't want to hurt his feelings, or to reject him. Isn't that pitiful? I agreed to marry a man I didn't even like, just because I didn't want him to feel bad. I think back on that now and I could slap me. But praise God for growth.

I believe God orchestrated that situation so that I would be forced to see some things about my personality. It's good to be a nice person. After all Jesus was gentle, kind and approachable. But there's no need to be a fool either. There is such a thing as being too nice. And I was being too nice. I was being weak. At the time, I didn't see it that way. I think I thought I was just doing the right thing, the thing that would make everyone happy. Thankfully I had a lot of praying people around me at the time. And none of them were saying anything. I kept wondering why. I kept asking for their advice. And nobody would say either yes I should marry him or no, I shouldn't. Especially not my mother. She left the decision completely up to me. I see now that God was using everyone's silence to force me to come to him directly to seek his opinion about this marriage. I think if there is one danger in growing up in a Christian home or Christian community it is this: It's really easy to rely on the opinions of your parents, aunts, uncles, siblings, cousins and friends, instead of seeking God himself for answers to your problems. Not that you should ignore the people God has put in your life. They're present for a reason. God often uses them to give wise counsel. But it's easy to develop the habit of substituting them for God. It's pretty easy to do because they know him, too. They live right. They know his word. Most of the time, they give extremely wise advice. But in the end, your relationship with God is yours alone. And you have to take responsibility for cultivating it. You have to pray to God yourself, not just coast on the prayers of loved ones. You must read your bible with your own two eyes, not just go on what your pastor teaches on Sundays. And most importantly, you've got to listen for and be obedient to the promptings of the Holy Spirit. So to make a long story short, I asked God what he wanted, and he made it clear that this guy was not my beloved. True to my passive nature, I called off the wedding, but not the relationship. We continued to date for a short while, until I finally called that off, too. This guy was so pushy that he declared that I couldn't break up with him without telling him why. I never did.

Everything was fine until I started dating another guy. He was fun to be around. He was outgoing. He had a nice job. He was in the church. He was a preacher's kid. Oh, and did I mention he was really gorgeous? But again, he was another dominant personality. We got along all right. Mainly because I never asserted myself. We went pretty much where he wanted to go. We did pretty much the things he wanted to do. I was just so passive. I never wanted to make any waves. I wanted to be a peace-maker. I didn't want to risk making anybody mad. In truth, I was just a coward. But I wasn't ready to see that yet. Anyway, he asked me to marry him, too! And I knew that I wasn't ready because I had just gotten out of the other relationship. The first time he asked I told him that I wasn't sure. But when he asked again, I just went on ahead and said yes! Can you believe that? You would have thought that I had learned my lesson the first time. But thank God. He will give you the same test over and over until you pass it. Obviously he needed to carve out some more character in me. And he used this scenario to do just that.

This time it was harder because of his lineage and his good looks. People said things to me like, "Girl, he's fine!" "He got a good job!" "You better not let him get away!" Everyone had an opinion, everyone except my family. Don't get me wrong, my relatives told me that they supported the union. But I could tell by their actions that they didn't. So there I went again trying to get an answer from everyone except God! Actually, right after I accepted the proposal, I did ask God if I had done the right thing. When I didn't hear anything I got really scared. So again, I tried to substitute my family's opinion for God's. And I felt so foolish! In the course of less than a year, I had been engaged twice! I must have looked crazy, walking around with an engagement ring on my finger, talking again about getting married. I wanted somebody, in no uncertain terms, to tell me what to do. Then one day, this older, praying woman at my church came to me and said "God has opened a door for you. It's up to you if you walk through it or not." I didn't know what the heck that meant! Did she mean marry him or don't marry him? Her words were so cloudy, they made no sense to me. My pastor, however, was a bit clearer. He said that I should just wait. And I did. The longer I waited, the less I wanted to marry. That's when I redis-covered my favorite scripture. Proverbs 3:5,6 It says, "Trust in the Lord with all thine heart and lean not to your own understanding. In all your ways acknowledge him and he will direct your path." I prayed that scripture everyday, crying, sometimes sobbing. Now you would have thought that common sense would have told me that if I had to go through all of that drama, that this guy must not be the one. But God patiently held my hand through it all. And as I sought him, he was faithful. After I arrived at the decision to call off the wedding, I experienced such a peace that I knew I had made the right choice. The only other emotion I felt was embarrassment. I just felt like such a dunce. And I know I looked so silly. I wanted to move to New York to get away, just so I wouldn't have to look at anybody I knew. Eventually, I got over my embarrassment. But I never forgot the lesson I learned. Even though I am still a mellow person, I am much more assertive in my decision-making. Most importantly, I always seek God first before I decide anything! His ways are best. He is never wrong. He has healed me from my need to please other people before pleasing him. Because he's got me, I know that whatever he wants me to do will succeed. So I don't fear the "what if's" because I know he has already made provision. And if somebody gets angry with me for doing what God told me to do? Oh well. That's their problem. Now my confidence is through the roof. But it's not in me, it's in him!

My advice to young ladies who struggle with any form of low self-esteem is to examine what God says about you. There is so much more to you than what you look like on the outside. Besides, God thinks you're beautiful! I can say that confidently, because God handmade you. Psalm 139 says that you are "fearfully and wonderfully made." That means that God handpicked every detail about you! Every detail! Can you believe that? Let me break it down for you. God wanted you so much that he allowed your parents to come together at the exact right moment in time in order for you to be created. If your dad's single sperm or your mom's single egg had been different, do you realize that you would not be you? You would be a totally different person. You truly are unique. A gift. A miracle! Please believe that. Although your parents participated in your procreation, God alone, sovereignly created you. He hand selected your hair texture, your hair color, your skin type, the shape of your eyes, the size of your nose and the shape of your feet, breasts and butt. And when he was all done, do you know what he did? He stood back, surveyed his work and said, "Beautiful!" If God thinks you're incredible, no one, (not even you) has a right to say anything different. Reject the lies of the enemy and embrace God's truth about you. You are beautiful. Love yourself!

Just as there is much more to you than what's on the outside, there's also so much more to you than what others think of you. Do you like who you are? Are you kind? Are you a good friend? Do you gossip? Can your friends trust you? Examine your relationship with God. Do you know him? Do you accept his opinion of you, or your friends instead? Are you following the guidelines he has laid out for your life? Or are you following the crowd?

If you don't know the Lord, take some time to pray this prayer:

> Lord Jesus, I need you. Please come into my heart right now and make me brand new. Forgive me for all of the bad things I have ever done. Help me to live right and to be the person you want me to be. I want every good thing that you have in store for me. Bless me, Lord and help me to stay on the right path. Amen.

If this is your first time praying this prayer, congratulations! You are saved! It really is just that easy. Salvation is a very personal decision between you and God. If you want to grow in your faith, here are some things you can do. First, find a church home. Look in your local yellow pages. Call one of the churches listed, tell them about your decision and check them out. See if any of them is a place you could call home. If you have a friend or relative who goes to church, try going with them. See if their church could become yours, too. But keep looking until you find some place that is a good fit, somewhere where you'll be challenged to grow and where you will learn more about Jesus Christ. Second, talk to someone who is a practicing Christian. It could be a friend, a relative or even a pastor. Tell them about your decision to follow Christ. Ask for their support. Ask them about their relationship with Christ. See what you learn.

If you are unable to pray this prayer now, don't worry. Just remember that the decision is up to you. Whenever you think you're ready, wherever you are, just ask Jesus to save you and he will.

God has created each of us with a special purpose. Knowing your purpose will also help to give you confidence. Experiencing God and his love will give you all the esteem you need. Just remember, if you look for God and ask him what He has planned for your life, you will find Him and He will tell you.

FOOD FOR THOUGHT:

Read Psalm 139:1-18

1. What do verses 13 through 18 tell you about how involved God was in your creation?

_____

_____

_____

2. What do verses 1 through 5 tell you about how well God knows your personality?

_____

_____

_____

_____

3. Do you believe that God thinks you're special? Why? Why not?

_____

_____

_____

_____

_____

_____

4. Say this: "I am 'fearfully and wonderfully made. Marvelous are your works and that my soul knows very well.' I love me!"

Someone tell me what's wron
Why my nights last so lon
It's getting hard to believe
at you ca... ...me. Then
me a s... ...you hear
nd let ...ark n

"Yes,
I am an
artist.
But I
am a
wife
first."

The Women

CHAPTER TWO

Erica

I tend to be an easy-going, laid back, mellow person. I pretty much go with the flow. I don't make too many demands. I don't make a lot of trouble, not because I'm afraid to or because I'm lazy. It's just that not a lot of things really bother me. Years ago, my father gave me the nickname "La dee da," because I just tend to take things as they come. I enjoy taking on the role of nurturer. I love to pamper my husband and to make him feel special. I like to cook and to take care of our home. I don't get to indulge that part of my personality very often though, because I keep a pretty hectic schedule, which keeps me away from home a lot.

When I have the time, my favorite things to do are read, spend time with my family and to watch as many home improvement shows as time will allow. I watch just about every design show on HGTV, the DIY network and the Style channel. I'm a fan of the "Christopher Lowell Show", "Bob Villa's Home Again" on the Discovery channel as well as of "Trading Spaces" on The Learning Channel. I enjoy these shows because I like to watch the transformation of an old, boring room into something new and beautiful. I love to see people's reactions to their new environment, too. I know how good I feel when I come into a room that's been redone, whether it has been painted or even if it's just the addition of something small, like a new comforter! I'm like, "Oooh! Pretty!" In my mind, I'm going to build my children's dream play area (whenever I have children). So I'm preparing myself by watching all the HGTV I can. I also want to remodel my mom's house.

I don't get to spend as much time with my family as I'd like. Not just because of my hectic schedule, but because of theirs. Everybody is always off doing something. It's hard to pin down so many people at one time. We try to schedule get-togethers of some kind at least once a month. It doesn't matter if it's something as big as a party, going to my mom's house or just going to the movies, as long as we get to see each other.

My dream is to get them all to come away to a log cabin in the woods, but I know that will never happen. I might be able to get one of my sisters to come (my younger sister, Alana), but that's about it. My husband is definitely out. Once on a camping trip, a bear invaded his cabin. I guess that was enough wildlife experience for him. I enjoy nature because it's a good way to get in touch with God's creation. It's peaceful. And whenever I go, I feel enormously grateful. I look around at the beauty of it all and think how awesome God must be to have created the earth so perfectly, to keep it all in balance and still be able to love me at the same time. It just blows me away. But like I said, I'll be blown away all by myself, because nobody else is feeling me.

I enjoy reading as well. I read a lot of self-help books and religious fiction. Although currently on my list is Cedric the Entertainer's book, which is not self-help, religious or fictional. I hear it's really funny though.

I definitely want to have children. I want a nice-sized family. Not as big as the one I grew up in. But I'd be happy with four children. I can't wait. I love babies! I often think about what my mom did for all of us. Honestly I don't know how she did it! But I know that when it's my time, God will give me all the grace I need to be effective. I guess that's what being a woman is all about.

I look to my mom and my mother-in-law as the best examples of womanhood. I want to be able to hold it down as well as they did in every area. Mothers are the center of the home. A good mom completes her duties pretty much unnoticed. When she's there, everything runs smoothly. But when she gets sick, or has to go out of town? The whole house falls apart because she's so much in the details. Dad can be sick and we'll roll with it. Kids get sick all the time. That's all right. But watch out if something happens to mom! The house will be in chaos because nobody knows what to do. That's how I want to be. I want to be the love, the bond, the strength, the nurturer. I want to be God's woman, not lacking in any area. I used to hear the song, "God's Woman," so much and never really think about it. But it has taken on much more significance as I've gotten older.

The world puts a lot of emphasis on looking good. And I want that, too. But I want it to be from the inside out. I want to be like the virtuous woman in Proverbs 31, walking so much in my purpose that every area of my life is exceptional. My marriage, motherhood, career, hobbies, ministry, I want all of them to be in order and pleasing to God. I want people to see a woman who knows her place in the world. I want them to see not only that I'm healthy not just because I want to look good, but because I am a good steward over my body. I want the world to see a woman who loves herself, feels good about herself, because God created her beautiful. I want to be a testament to other women of God's faithfulness, so that they can see the truth of Philippians 4:13. "I can do all things through Jesus Christ who strengthens me."

I want my husband to be able to say about me that I am his best friend. I want us to stay the kind of best friends that even if we're mad at one another, we'll still talk and tease each other. We're kind of like little kids in that way…almost like brother and sister in how comfortable we are with each other and sometimes in how we relate to each other. Nobody can get under my skin as much as Warryn can. But that's because I love him more than anyone else.

Warryn and I are in such a unique position because we work so closely together. It can be real "special" sometimes. We've learned to work together well. But I haven't learned not to take his constructive criticism personally. If he says "I don't like this," or "Change that," or "Fix this," I get upset. Mainly it's because I put so much of myself into what I create, that when he rejects it, he rejects a part of me. I get so attached to what I sing and what I write. So when he tells me that it's not good, I don't say "Okay, well let's make it better." I should, but I don't. I just get my feelings hurt. The funny thing is that he'll be over it and will have moved on to something else, but I'll still be pouting, holding us up. I know it's sad. But give me a break. I'm a work in progress, too. Ultimately I know that he's just trying to get the best out of Tina and me, so it's cool.

Our relationship is so precious to me. We are each other's best friends & we love spending time together.

The fact that Warryn produces us means that I do get to see him more often than if he didn't work with us at all, a fact that Tina is ever so quick to point out. She tells me that it's not fair that I get to see Warryn so often, when she hardly gets to see Teddy at all. But I have to remind her that when we're working, my husband does not act very husband-like. In the studio, he's Mr. Campbell, "Baby Dub," working with Mary Mary. Ain't no Warryn and Erica going on.

Work is so much a part of who we are as a couple, that it's sometimes difficult not to bring it home with us. We try not to – but we don't do a very good job. I've been singing since I was five. He started tinkering on the drums when he was two. Our challenge is learning how to make a distinction between music and our life despite the fact that music is our life! We had a discussion about this very thing early

23

on in our marriage. Warryn said that he knew how we could separate the two. He suggested that we just not talk about business. I agreed. Our resolve lasted for about two minutes. It was almost impossible! Still we continue to try. I don't ever want to feel like I'm living with my producer. When I'm home, I want to be with my husband and he wants to be with his wife. It is a challenge, but we try to carve out private time.

It's funny too. Some days we'll be together and it's obvious that we're trying not to bring up the album, the song, radio airplay, some performance or something. We're getting better at making the distinction if for no other reason than we don't want our marriage to turn into one big work day. When I return from touring or a concert date, I always try to do something wifely. I'll cook something; do laundry – engage in something totally unrelated to Mary Mary. I want to make the statement, "Yes, I am an artist. But I am your wife first."

I also have concerns about the fact that marriages between entertainers don't seem to work out. Divorce is not an option for us, but then neither is a loveless, dried up "arrangement." I refuse to settle for a poor imitation of a marriage. I know with all my being that Warryn is the man that God handpicked for me. Our relationship is so precious to me. We are each other's best friends and we love spending time together. Our relationship is only deepened by our faith in the Lord. We don't depend on our own resources or even our own emotions in order to love one another. I know enough to know that human resources are finite and emotions change. God is our Anchor, our Third Strand in the "cord not easily broken," our Source, our Guide. His word is our manual for marriage, for managing our careers, for loving our families, for life!

Not long ago, I was going through a really rough time. I was anxious and trying not to worry. Warryn called me up and ministered God's word to me! It was incredible! It was the kind of word you might expect to get from your pastor or from a discipleship leader. Except it came from my husband! I was so encouraged; I perked right up. My whole attitude changed toward my problem. I was ready to face it and I knew that it wasn't going to be that bad. That's what I'm talking about! I got me a man that loves him some Jesus and can deliver a word to his wife! It is such a blessing to be able to love someone, work with him, be his best friend and to have him encourage you spiritually. That puts your relationship on a whole new level. I love it!

If you are married, and especially if you work closely together, set aside time just for the two of you. If you have children, get a baby sitter; call on a grandparent, a neighbor or somebody responsible. Be sure to make your spouse feel special as often as you can. Pursue your romantic fantasies. Take a trip. If you can't go far, or stay away for long, then rent a room at a nice hotel for a weekend. Decorate your bedroom. Light candles. Take a bath together. Attend a marriage conference. Renew your vows. Your marriage needs to feel special, not regular. Encourage one another. Pray for each other. Pray together when it's possible. Keep God at the center of your relationship and seek him together. If anything is missing, he can give you what you need to restore, refresh or renew yourselves.

So I had all of these preconceived notions about what the ideal guy for me looked like, never knowing that the whole time, Teddy was perfectly made for me.

Tina

Working closely with my sister can be a lot like working with a spouse. I love working with Erica because she's my best friend outside of my husband. She loves me. She's concerned about me. She wants the best for me. That's the best kind of person to be in partnership with. But like spouses, sisters fuss and fight about silly things that they wouldn't even mention if they were working with a stranger. Sometimes Erica and I can't avoid those spots. I think we could definitely stand to be more considerate of one another. We could treat each other with the same consideration that we would give to a non-family member that we wanted to make a good impression on. We could also practice a little more (hint hint).

The best part about getting to work with your sister is that it's so much fun! Erica and I have a good time wherever we go. We're constantly laughing at our own inside jokes. After all of the crazy, terrible moments that you have as a performer, the times that make you think that you just can't take this anymore, the sister element – reminiscing, remembering that you're family, and knowing that your relationship is bigger than all of this enables you to laugh at any situation and to keep on moving. There's nothing like it. The fact that I love Erica as much as I love my life, the fact that I'm really concerned about her and that I want our relationship as sisters to be right before anything else, that's what keeps us grounded and this career of ours in proper perspective. Erica is truly a godly woman.

She fits my definition of womanhood. To me a woman is strong, yet gentle. She perseveres, creates a loving atmosphere, helps to maintain stability, fears God, loves God, respects her husband, cares for him, and keeps the home happy and peaceful. Erica pretty much does all of those things.

I began to see myself as a woman about three years ago, when I realized that my values had changed. The things that had been important to me in high school and at the start of college just suddenly weren't. In high school and college, I had been concerned with all of the external things: what kind of car I drove, the clothes I wore, whether or not it seemed like I had it going on or not. Then my attitude shifted. I became more concerned with family and with becoming a good person. I began to realize that no matter what kind of person I was, I would have an effect on the world around me directly or indirectly. I began to think about what kind of wife I would be and what kind of mother would I make, even though I wasn't even married yet. Looking at the examples around me, I saw that a mother sets the tone for the whole household. If she's loving, peaceful, understanding, a caretaker, who lives her life with integrity, then her home will reflect that. Likewise, if she is messy, mean, unorganized, selfish and uncaring, her home will reflect that, too. I started to see myself further on down the line and decided the type of woman I wanted to become. I was beginning to see that pleasing my friends and impressing strangers was nowhere as important as becoming the woman God wanted me to be. I began to build my assets, making sure that I was financially secure, even if I didn't look like it. I became more aware about decisions I made concerning my career. I made better investments, not just with my money, but with my time. I began to focus more on self-improvement, perfecting myself according to God's principles, which are the essence of life. Living the way God wants me to, makes it possible for me to make a difference in the world at large, and among the people closer to me. I learned to be content with myself by gaining a better understanding of my greater purpose. I mentioned that when I started to focus on improving myself that I wasn't married yet. I think that's important. I believe that God was preparing me to become a wife and (one day) a mother. My husband, Teddy Campbell, and I met on the road doing gospel stage plays. Let me back up…Prior to leaving to go on the road, my sisters and I were participating in a recording session, singing background vocals for a particular young lady. The music director of the play was producing the session. He was a friend of Teddy's, who was also the drummer for the same play. Teddy just happened to be at the session. Once it ended, as my sisters and I were leaving, the music director invited us to another play that he and Teddy were doing that same night. As I walked off the set, Teddy said, loudly enough for me to hear, "Please bring her (meaning me) tonight." I told him to calm down or something silly like that. And that was how we met.

When we got out on the road, I was so focused on work, that I was doing my best to ignore him as a potential boyfriend. I did not want to start a relationship. I did not want to be in a relationship. I didn't even want to hear about a relationship. I didn't want anything to interfere with my work. And beyond not wanting a relationship, I really didn't want one with him, because he did not fit the criteria for my "ideal" man. He wasn't what I thought I wanted (key word being "thought"). He wasn't a big, giant basketball player-type guy. He wasn't extra studious or super sophisticated (which, by the way, neither am I!). Not to mention a guy like that couldn't even understand me – not even a little bit. I possess some of those characteristics, but they don't jump out at you when you meet me. I'm crazy, fun-loving. I brighten a room. I talk a lot. I want to know everything. I make room for myself if there is none. Don't ask me why I thought I wanted an extra-studious and super sophisticated guy. Maybe I developed the idea sometime in childhood or as a teenager, like lots of girls do. Sort of the same way everybody wants to grow up to be a doctor, a lawyer or a firefighter because that's all they know, then they discover other talents and interests they'd rather pursue. But to do that, they have to give up on becoming a doctor, a lawyer or firefighter. Like many women, as I matured, I had to learn that being happy at the end of the day is much more important than being concerned about how perfect your situation appears to be.

So I had all of these preconceived notions about what the ideal guy for me looked like, never knowing that the whole time, Teddy was perfectly made for me. I got to know him better while we were on the road. He was mad cool…just like me. He was fun-loving, crazy, sincere, genuine, upbeat. He was my same age. Everyone else was older and stiffer. I could relate to him. I enjoyed his friendship. But all the while I was telling myself, "You don't like him like that, right?" Well, after the play ended, I found out just how much I liked him. I sat in the airport waiting for my plane to Southern California, just crying. I mean just weeping, still talking about "But I don't want like him like that." Whatever.

It must have been mutual, because two days later he called me from his hometown of Chicago. He said, "Do you want me to come out there?" And I was like, "Yes!" He flew out for a visit. And we've been a couple ever since. We did the long distance thing for three years before he moved out to California permanently. Then two years later we got married. What's so funny is that even when he moved out, I wasn't thinking marriage. I just knew that we were in a great relationship and that I loved him and that I didn't want it to end. I know this sounds unbelievable, but four years into our relationship, is when it dawned on me that Teddy was perfect for me. I knew he loved me for me. He understood me. We had enough similarities to be in sync with each other and enough differences to balance each other. I knew he wasn't a perfect man. But he was perfect for me. He must have sensed it or something, because shortly after this revelation, he asked me to marry him. I have to tell you how he proposed. It was so cute!

Teddy Campbell proposed to me on February 15, 1999. I remember the date because it was the day after Valentine's Day. The day before we had both been working. I had been singing background for Kenny Lattimore, while Teddy had been playing the drums for Gerald Lavert or someone like that. We met up in Chicago for what had to be the most perfect date of all time. He picked me up and took me to lunch in a restaurant in the Sears Tower. Then we went to the top. The weather was so clear, you could see almost to Detroit. It seemed like you could see all the way to California; it was so beautiful. We had our picture taken and walked around a little. It was just a blissful day. He took me back to my hotel, and I'm thinking he's going to head home or whatever, but no. He walks me to my room, which he had already checked me into, and opens the door. I can't even describe the sight. There were candles everywhere. There was fruit set out on a tray. The whole room just radiated an atmosphere of love. Then he blindfolded me and sat me down. I cooperated. When he started feeding me pieces of fruit, asking me to identify them, part of me was thinking how romantic this was. But another part of me was like, "What the crap is going on, here?" So there I am, talking about, "That's an orange. That's strawberry. That's a banana. That's a grape." Then he put something metal just between my teeth so I could bite down on it a little. And I'm going, "This is a...this is a..." Meanwhile, I'm still zoned out. It has not registered that this is a marriage proposal. I'm thinking, how cute that he's giving me a promise ring! Then when he took off the blindfold, and I saw him on his knees, it still didn't register...I haven't yet put it together that the day had been just full of bliss, that everything had gone perfectly, that it had all been so romantic. Then he started to tell me how I was the best part of his life; how he couldn't imagine life without me; he knows who I am; and he would love to spend the rest of his life with me...Believe it or not, I still think I'm getting a promise ring. Then when he said, "Will you marry me?" I just started to cry. Of course I said yes. And the rest, as they say, is history.

Although when Teddy went downstairs to get my bags, I did call my Uncle, Pastor Charles Edward Lollis, to get his blessing. He's the most discriminating man I know. He has always lived a godly life and walked upright before me. He's not easily won over and speaks only the truth. People think he's hard on folks sometimes, but my opinion is that he's sincere and is unafraid to say the hard things that people need to hear. He had only met Teddy a few times, but I knew it had been enough to determine how he felt about my fiancé. I value his opinion so much, that had he even hesitated, I would have had to reconsider Teddy's proposal. So when Uncle Charles said that Teddy was a good man; that he'd make a fine husband, and that he himself was really happy for me, I fell even deeper in love. I know when Teddy got back with my bags, he must have noticed that I was even peppier! He just didn't know...I was relieved and excited!

We totally give God credit for our success! We know of too many people who've been trying to get signed for forty years...here it only took us a short time! It's Amazing.

"...we were forced to choose between going after our dream without any connections, hook-ups or contacts to speak of, or we could get "real" jobs."

Another person whose hesitation would have caused me to rethink my decision is my mother. I trust her opinions completely in everything. She is a woman of God. She has always stood for something good. She is one of the best examples of what it means to be a woman. She's a good person. She is for peace. She is for what's right. She raised us with the fear of God and of her and my dad. We definitely had a little fear of my parents because we didn't want to feel their wrath. By the same token, as we got older and became adults, they allowed us to make our own decisions. They would give us advice, but left the choices up to us. They didn't try to manipulate us into the direction they thought we should take, even if it was obviously the right one. They trusted their upbringing of us. They also trusted us to make wise decisions. Most importantly, they trusted God to watch over and convict us if necessary. If we were doing something completely out of pocket, they might say a little something just to make us think about what we were doing. But they never forbade us to do anything, tried to control our lives. In short, they never tried to step into the role of God in our lives.

Now don't get me wrong, when we were little, our parents were God of our house. We could make a few choices, but that was it. My parents were the parents – straight up. We kids ran nothing. When we got older, they allowed us to be adults, which meant being responsible for our own choices. And because my mother never involved herself in all of my decisions, but set an incredible example of godliness for me to follow, her opinion carried a lot of weight. What she felt about my life and my decisions still mean the world to me. I have always trusted that she would tell me only what she thought was right, not just what she wanted me to do. So when she said, "Oh baby, that's good. And I think Teddy's going to be a wonderful husband. I see something in him I like. He's a good person," I knew I had the right guy.

FOOD FOR THOUGHT:

Read Proverbs 31:10-31
1. According to this scripture, what are the characteristics of a virtuous woman?

_____

_____

_____

_____

_____

_____

_____

_____

2. Define "virtue" in your own words. Is virtue a relevant character trait or is it too "old fash-ioned" to apply to girls and women today? Why?

_____

_____

_____

_____

_____

_____

_____

_____

_____

_____

_____

_____

_____

_____

_____

_____

_____

_____

_____

_____

_____

_____

_____

3. What can you do to become more virtuous in your own life?

_____

_____

_____

_____

_____

_____

_____

_____

_____

_____

_____

_____

_____

_____

_____

_____

_____

_____

_____

_____

_____

_____

_____

_____

_____

4. *Pray this: "Dear Father, show me how I can become a girl/young*
   adult/woman who will make you proud."

_____

_____

_____

_____

_____

_____

_____

_____

_____

_____

_____

_____

_____

_____

_____

_____

_____

_____

_____

_____

_____

_____

_____

The Artists

CHAPTER THREE

Erica

Tina and I have been singing since we were fifteen and five years old, respectively. At fifteen and eleven we joined the choir at our church. By ages sixteen and eleven we were performing solos. We never thought that we would sing anywhere else but in our church choir. Of course, we sang all the time at home and at some family functions. But it never entered our minds to do it for a living. As a matter of fact, Tina thought that she would become a school teacher. I became a cosmetologist. As a hobby, Tina started dabbling in make-up. Between the two of us, we would experiment on each other. People at church would notice that we had a special little something going on. They would often comment on how we styled our hair and applied our make-up. Even with their comments, we still never thought of it leading anywhere near entertainment. Hair and make-up were just things that we did. Then one day, something happened.

A friend told me about auditions for a stage play, called "Mama I'm Sorry," starring Melba Moore. She had heard me sing and encouraged me to try out. I thought that I wasn't good enough to sing on stage, but I ended up going anyway. Tina went with me for support. To my surprise, when I finished singing, the director asked me for my availability! This was my first audition for anything, and I had been hired on the spot! Not wanting to go on the road alone, I quickly told him that Tina could sing, too! 'Cause I wasn't going without my sister. He listened to her and hired her, right then and there! Just like that, we were on the Gospel Play Circuit.

For those of you who are unfamiliar with it, The Gospel Play Circuit is a series of plays and musicals that tour the U.S. for about a year at a time. The producers, actors and stagehands are mostly black folks who enjoy the theatre, but for whom, performing on Broadway is not usually an option. Financially speaking, the productions tend to be lower end, but not lacking in talent or professionalism. As such, the circuit boasts few conveniences. As performers, Tina and I did just about everything except drive the bus. All of the actors did our own hair, make-up, wardrobe, and programs. We were all understudies for nearly every part. You name it; we did it. As you may have guessed, it wasn't the highest paying job in the world, but it was the best experience for a new performer. It was taxing work, but it taught me so much about performing, and the business behind it. I am very grateful to have had that experience so early on in my life and in my career.

After our first show, I was hooked. I found the touring exhilarating. I loved the thrill of visiting a new city every month! I enjoyed performing before a live audience. For the twelve months that we toured, I was in heaven. I knew that I had discovered my calling. How I was going to get from singing in a small play to singing professionally, I had no idea. I didn't care, I just wanted to do it.

I soon saw the down side of life as an entertainer. When the show's run ended, we were back at home without jobs and with no means of income. We hadn't made that much money doing the play to begin

For so long he's been waiting everyday anticipating for you to realize...

that he's so close to you

Tina

After we came back home from doing "Mama I'm Sorry," we knew that we wanted to sing for a living. The entertainment bug had bitten us bad. We wanted "in" on the recording industry, but we had no leads to speak of. While we were touring, we had met Warryn Campbell (now Erica's husband and my brother-in-law), who at that time had been playing keyboards for Brandy. Once we all got back to southern California, a mutual friend of ours and Warryn's invited us to come hang out at Warryn's house. We would hang out with him often, just singing church songs, changing up lyrics, beats and melodies. We were just a bunch of church kids, who just loved to make music. So we'd be having these "jam" sessions, for lack of a better word, writing and singing just for fun. Now because we were just hanging out, it never entered my mind or Erica's that we should ask Warryn to help us get a deal, or even to make a demo. It probably should have, but it didn't. For Erica it was a little bit more complicated. She really liked Warryn and didn't want him to think that she was using him. As a matter of fact, she never mentioned to him how bad she wanted to become a recording artist until after they were married. We just wanted to tinker with some songs and create music. So we never gave it a second thought. Our fun and tinkering evolved into a little writing coalition that started with "What a Friend," which is on our "Thankful" C.D. I had actually written the song four years before I shared it with Warryn. After he heard it, he made some changes, added some of his ideas and some of his production expertise and turned it into something better and more beautiful. Music just flowed from us as a hobby. We had no idea that it could or would actually go somewhere. Later, one of our songs got into the hands of EMI publishing, ended up on the "Doctor Dolittle II" soundtrack, and we ended up getting a deal. That's the short version.

The more detailed version goes something like this. At the time, Warryn was being managed by Kenneth Creer of The Firm in Beverly Hills. Kenneth was attending a meeting in New York with some Columbia executives on behalf of another client, who had no connections to Warryn. While he was in that meeting, another Columbia executive passed through – just passed through now – and urged Kenneth to stop talking about this other client and to play the Mary Mary song! The other executives listened and liked the demo so much that the meeting ceased to be about the other client and became a Mary Mary meeting, even though Kenneth did not represent us (yet)! Isn't that something? God used that executive, who was just passing through to get us noticed. Columbia called us right away; we flew out shortly after. We liked their offer so we looked it over with our lawyer to be sure that we liked it. We did, so we and signed on the dotted line! Isn't God amazing? Just like that we had a deal. What makes it more incredible is that we found out later from Warryn that he had been trying to shop our songs to other music executives, but kept getting the doors slammed in his face. It turns out they didn't know what to do with gospel singers with our kind of sound. But God knew exactly where he wanted us to be. And he made everything work together so that we could get the blessing He had set aside just for us. And as it often happens in this business, once Columbia had expressed an interest in us, then others became interested, too. They still didn't know what to do with us, but they were willing to give it a try. We went from having no deal to having major record companies wanting us. Now it's all God and it's all good. Praise God!

We totally give God credit for our success! We know of too many people who've been trying to get signed for forty years or something ridiculous like that, and are still trying! And here it only took us a short time! I can't explain it, except to say that God decided it was our time. So when other artists talk about how God had nothing to do with their deal, I just listen. Because truthfully, he may not have had anything to do with their getting signed, but I know he was totally responsible for our deal! We couldn't have created a better chain of events, even if we had known how! For whatever reason, God just gave us favor and we got our record deal. They could hear what none of those other executives could! So began the saga of Mary Mary.

Of course once you get signed, then the real work starts. You're under pressure now to deliver on the record label's investment in you. You've stepped out on a limb now and must back up all that faith talk with action. When we left our regular, paying jobs, we had no idea what we were getting ourselves into. There is just so much that isn't guaranteed in this business. Once you get signed, you may get your little advance, but even that has to be paid back out of your record sales. People don't realize how much faith it takes to step off into this line of work. Artists can look all glammed up with their hair coiffed, their make-up done, new white teeth and fabulous clothes, but in truth they can be totally broke!

An advance does not equal security. We had a deal. Our faces were everywhere. Our videos were playing on BET. We looked like we had it going on! Folks thought we were all Hollywood and living the highlife. But at some point, we didn't even have enough money to pay our rent. Revenues from things we had put in place just weren't coming through. Suddenly that job I had five years ago, earning $21,000 a year wasn't looking so bad anymore.

That's the nature of this business. You are constantly selling yourself (not literally – not like prostitution or anything like that…although some artists, like Prince, have compared it to slavery…well paid slavery, but slavery nonetheless), your image, your style, your music. And the rules are real clear. Like Paul said, if you don't work, you don't eat. It's just that simple. So we set out to do the promotion and marketing things…the in-store appearances, the radio shows, the talk shows, the concerts, the gospel showcases, anything that would help the world to know who we were and to hear our songs. It's fun work, but it's hard work sometimes, too. There are artists who don't have to work as hard now, like Michael Jackson, Tina Turner and a few others. But those people are legends! They are at the point in their careers where if they chose not to, they wouldn't have to work another day in their lives and they'd still be able to live extremely well. Mary Mary may get to that point one day, but that's not where we are now.

Honestly, I don't know that it's our goal to get to the point of retirement. We wouldn't mind financial prosperity, of course, but Mammon doesn't guide our career choices, the Holy Spirit does. So even if we sold 100 billion copies of our current album and could retire and live comfy for the rest of our lives, we wouldn't do it unless the Holy Spirit specifically told us to. By the same token, even if we couldn't give an album away and God said to keep going, that's what we would do. Our writing, singing and performing is not just a career for us. It's a ministry. And in ministry you have One Boss and what He says goes. So until God tells us differently, we're in this music thing for the long haul. As long as God continues to open doors, we'll continue to walk through them. We have every confidence in His person and we will obey Him, whatever He tells us to do.

So like I said, we went though a really tough financial crunch for a minute. I was thinking "I'm going to have to start cuttin' some grass, sellin' some newspapers, doin' some make-up or somethin' to bring in some cash!" (I'm being extreme of course) But then things began to look up. As a matter of fact, our first year was almost like a fairy tale. We were the darlings of the industry. Everybody was playing our music; we were making a lot of appearances; our faces seemed to be everywhere; our sales were great; we were nominated for and won a Grammy for Best Contemporary Gospel Album. Among other awards, we also won a Lady of Soul music award. And not just for Best New Gospel Artist, but for Best New Artist! That was really incredible and important, too.

The two little girls from Inglewood had made good.
You couldn't tell us nothing about what God was able to do.

We had gotten engulfed by this new world of music and listening to the advice of all the experts about what needed to be done to get and to keep Mary Mary on top. Let me make it clear that it's not a bad thing to take the advice of experts

Let me take a minute to speak on that. People often try to pigeon-hole you by limiting you to categories. We are gospel, but we wanted to be acknowledged as a group that makes good music across the board. We didn't want people to say "Oh! That's a good gospel song." We wanted them to say, "That's a good song!" Period. Because if a song is great, it shouldn't matter if it's country, gospel, R&B or pop. A good song is just a good song. Likewise, a good group is a just good group. Period. And that's how we wanted to be acknowledged. Winning the award for Best New Artists at the Lady of Soul Awards confirmed for us that our music had hit the mark.

Continuing on...We were really doing this thing! The two little girls from Inglewood had made good. You couldn't tell us nothing about what God was able to do. As far as production and getting the first album, "Thankful," out, things could have gone a lot more smoothly, but for a freshman effort, overall it went really well. And "Thankful"'s reception by the public exceeded our expectations! We were blown away when it went platinum! We had high expectations, but God exceeded our expectations by far. We knew we had good material, but when you're doing a new thing, you never know how people will feel about it. Our music is definitely hip hop and soul, but our message is the Gospel of Jesus Christ. So since we didn't necessarily sound like or look like traditional gospel artists, we weren't exactly sure how people would take to our sound, our look, or our lyrics. We were just hoping that there were some people out there who felt the same way we did, people who liked hip hop ans soul, but who wanted some sanctified, inspiring lyrics to go with the phat beats. So we stepped out on faith, and God took care of the rest!

If our first effort was heavenly, then our second effort was hellish! For our sophomore effort, "Incredible," it felt like we were living out the lyrics to our song "Shackles." "Everything that could go wrong all went wrong at one time." I can't go into great detail, but everything that was supposed to happen, either got delayed or canceled. Everything that was supposed to go right went left. Everybody who was supposed to be in place was out of place or gone. The CD was supposed to drop in August of 2001, but it didn't come out until July of 2002. Things that were in place to keep finances current, fell through. Key people that we needed, in order to ensure that our project was top notch, dropped out. We were thinking that it just don't take all of this to be saved. And that job I had five years ago, making $21,000 began to look even better. That was bad enough. But remember family is real important to us. It's everything. I can put up with a lot if my family is straight. Well even our family came under attack! Our personal lives took a drastic turn when our daddy's condition started acting up again, resulting in his being hospitalized three times in one year! At one point we were out on the road, touring, while our father lay in' a coma in the hospital! It felt like everything was falling apart. There we were ministering to people about holding on, thinking "Okay God I know you not gon' let my Daddy die, while I'm doing your work, right?" I know that's cheeky, because of course, God can do whatever he wants without anyone's permission and it's always good. But at the time, we just wanted him to keep our daddy alive.

We stayed in God's face. Where else could we go? Who else could work out this mess? It was tempting to throw a tantrum. But you know, really, what good would that have done? It wouldn't have solved anything. If you're broke and then go and have a nervous breakdown, guess what? When you return to your sane mind and open your eyes, you still ain't go no money in the bank! If somebody gets sick and in your grief, you pass out and they have to send an ambulance for you, too? When you wake up, you'll be in the hospital, laying right next to that first person who got sick. And you know what? Your fainting spell won't have improved their health one bit. So you may as well kill the drama, pull it together and do something useful, like pray. God is the only One who can help you in times of crisis. Jesus knows a little something about being abandoned, grieved to the point of death and facing a really deadly situation.

So we began asking God what happened. Had we done something wrong? Were we out of order? We didn't necessarily believe that he was punishing us, as much as we believed that the enemy was attacking us. But even if that was so, our Heavenly Father had allowed it to happen for a reason. And although his ways are not our ways, they are always for our good. We wanted to know what we were supposed to learn from this experience. We desperately wanted his perspective on what was going on. So we started by prayerfully examining our thoughts, attitudes and actions. We discerned that one major lesson that God was trying to teach us was that we had begun to place our trust in all the wrong things. He had been so faithful to us our entire lives. He was the one who had seen our family through poverty, illness and death. He alone had orchestrated our lives so that we were put in a position to get a record deal in the first place. And all by himself, He had given us favor with executives and with our fans. Here He had done all of this and so much more, and we were trippin.'

We had gotten engulfed by this new world of music and listening to the advice of all the experts about what needed to be done to get and to keep Mary Mary on top. Let me make it clear that it's not a bad thing to take the advice of experts. The word says that in "the midst of wise counsel there is great safety." But we had made the mistake of trusting in that advice and in the people who gave it more than in God. We had placed our faith in too many entities. Our faith couldn't be in the money that made up the budget. It shouldn't have been in the presence of this person, or in the expertise of that person, or in the availability of the other person. Our faith shouldn't have been in the fact that we had support from this group or from that company, or in the fact that we know we've got the money to back stuff up. Our faith should have been strictly in God. That was where we blew it.

When you have no means to get anything done, and I don't just mean financially, but when you don't even have hope because your situation looks so bad you don't have any hook-ups, connections, support – anything; when you don't have the means for whatever it takes to get what you're after in your life, whether it's a place to sleep, food or shelter for your family, a new job, any job, a record deal, a way to pay for college, finding a spouse, healing for your marriage, getting your kids off drugs, getting them or yourself out of jail, direction for your life, starting your own business or even just finding a true friend, when you put yourself in God's hands and try to live a life that's pleasing to Him, He will take care of you. He's so good and loves us so much that even if you're just raggedy and have totally screwed up and know that you are living foul, he will take care of you, if you reach out to him. At any time, you can ask him to pull you up and to set your feet on firmer ground. NowHe may not do it the way you think He should; He may not do it according to your timetable, but he will do it. He promises that. If you call on him in your hour of need, he will answer you. My entire family is living proof of that.

In this world, it's so easy to get caught up in the way people tell you things are "supposed to be done." When you put your hope in happenings, other people, situations, in things having to go a certain way, you automatically set yourself up for disaster. I guarantee that you will be let down. You will be disappointed. But when you put your trust in God, he gives you his peace in exchange for your problem. And his peace "just don't make no sense." It really is beyond human understanding. We should not have made it through this last year. And if we had continued to lean on our own understanding, and our own strength, we wouldn't have. Mary Mary as well as Tina and Erica would have been a thing of the past. But we placed our trust back in God alone, and he took care of us.

Our father was at the point of death. Everybody who had been working for us and with us had gone their own way. We faced trying to complete our project with none of the support that we had enjoyed the first year. And yet we had perfect peace. People who don't know Jesus sometimes think that when Christians talk about giving everything over to God that we're copping out; that we're refusing to deal with reality. That's not the case at all. When you really know God and you have experienced him personally, working things out in your life, why would you try to do it yourself? You could never do as good a job as he could. You don't have nearly the same amount of power he does. You don't know even a billionth of what he knows. All you are likely to do is mess things up more. You may have heard the old adage, "Give your problems to God; he's going to be up all night anyway." It's so true. When you find yourself in a situation that is completely beyond your control and understanding, or you have no hope, instead of trying to wrap your little, human brain around your problem, you may as well give it to God (who knows everything). No one else will be able to help you anyway. If you lack anything, call on Jehovah Jireh. If you or someone you love is sick, get to know God as your healer. If you are in trouble, know there is no situation too hard for God. He doesn't just have all you need; He is all that you need.You can't proclaim that for sure unless you experience it. Faith is not rational; it must be tested.

Trying to handle an impossible situation apart from God is how people end up stressed out, going crazy, committing suicide, addicted to drugs and alcohol, developing ulcers, and all other kinds of illnesses. God did not design our bodies, minds and spirits to live under stress for long periods of time. We can't handle that. But God can. Besides, who can relate to your problem better than Jesus? Only someone who has personally conquered death can give you the peace to deal with your drama. To him nothing is a surprise. We were shocked when things started to fall apart, but God wasn't. He knew about that year in our lives before either of us was ever born. And he had already made provision. That's what we had to remember.

So God saw us through that time in our lives and here we are writing a book about it! God healed our father. He restored our finances. He blessed us with new homes and a few other luxuries. Our family is fine. Our sophomore effort is being well received. We are happy in our careers and in our marriages. And we are keeping our focus on and our trust in him.

Erica

That was a difficult time. And even as we are gaining in popularity, like Tina said, we've got a long way to go. Of course, our family thinks that Mary Mary is everywhere and that the whole world knows who we are. To them we've always been super stars, since we started singing solos in the choir. But we've got work to do. And that's fine. We're up to the challenge. I prefer a slow crawl to a sudden jump any day. The work is hard. But it's work that I love even through its ups and downs. I love it, even when I'm stressed out, wondering if somebody is going to play our song on the radio or play our video. The cool thing is that during these times, God will always remind me of what's really important. Someone will come up to tell me how much they love our song, or how the lyrics we wrote touched them. At times like that I have to say "Wow God! Thank you for letting me do this for a living! Thank you for encouraging me!" So even though we have our professional goals and visions for our lives, we know what God has planned for us is so much bigger than what we can imagine and it concerns much more than record sales. If we just follow his path for us, stay close to him and stay focused on him, we'll be amazed at how he uses us for the kingdom. It will be all good.

FOOD FOR THOUGHT

Read Psalm 30:5, Romans 8:28, Galatians 6:9, James 1:2-4 and Psalm 139:16

1. Describe one of the most difficult times you have ever been through.

_____

_____

_____

_____

_____

_____

_____

_____

_____

_____

_____

_____

_____

_____

2. How did you handle it?

_____

_____

_____

_____

_____

3. What do the scriptures above tell you about God's perspective of hard times?

_____

_____

_____

_____

_____

4. Do this: The next time you go through a rough time, ask God to show you what he wants you to learn from it. Then examine your situation for his answer.

_____

_____

Erica

you thought you knew,

Erica Monique Campbell

Birthdate: April 29.

Place of Birth: Saint Francis Hospital, Lynwood, CA • High School Alma Mater: Lynwood High School
Height: 5'3" • Dress Size: Small • Hair Color: Dark Brown • Eye Color: Dark Brown
Favorite Scripture: Proverbs 3:5,6 • Desired Pet: Cockerspaniel •
Musical Influences: Commissioned, The Clark Sisters, The Winans •
Personal Influences: Mom, Meliea (older sister), Barbette (cousin)
Hobbies: Reading, spending time with family, watching home improvement shows

Greatest Heartbreak:
Being misunderstood,
especially when I
have the
best intentions

but you had no idea!

Favorite Book: The Left Behind Series • Favorite Performer: Kirk Franklin • Favorite Actor: Denzel

Washington • Favorite Movie: Monsters, Inc. • Favorite Author: Sister Souljah • Favorite Car:

BMW X5 • Favorite Designer: Roberto Covalli Jeans • Favorite Make-up Line: MAC • Favorite

Sound: Oleta Adams' Voice • Favorite Euphamism: "That's special" (read: ugly) • Hopes to hear

God say when she gets to heaven: Well done my good and faithful servant!

Greatest Hope:

That people
come to Christ
and experience an
enjoyable life

Pet Peeve: Fake, mean people • Favorite Profession (barring current one): Author of children's books • Least Favorite Profession: Working at the grocery store • Greatest Joy: Feeling loved Find confusing: People being mean without reason • Causes Great Anxiety: Some of the obligations that I must meet as a performer • Greatest Fear: That people don't get me Thing that most people would be surprised to know about her:
That sometimes I'm insecure

Mamma Atkins

Poppa Atkins

Before preforming in Amsterdam

Teddy my husband and
Cierra my daughter

At a radio station in Japan with fans.

Tina with Mother in Law

Grandma Daniels

Erica enjoys good times with her family

Girls with the parents

Erica, Tina, Kirk Franklin and Niko (hairstylist) on the set of the "Thank You" video for the "Kingdom Come" Soundtrack.

Tina

you thought you knew,

Trecina Evette Campbell
Birthdate: May 1.

Place of Birth: • Centinela Hospital, Inglewood, CA • High School Alma Mater: Morningside High School, Inglewood, CA • Height: 5'4" • Dress Size: Medium • Hair Color: Red • Eye Color: Hazel • Favorite Scripture: Proverbs 31:10 Desired Pet: A dog-not sure what kind • Greatest Musical Influences: Commissioned, The Clark Sisters, The Winans

Favorite Performer:
Pastor Shirley Caesar,
Mary J. Blige

but you had no idea!

Greatest Personal Influences: Aunt Theresa • Favorite Book: The Power of a Praying Wife •
Favorite Performer: Pastor Shirley Caesar, Mary J. Blige • Favorite Actor: Robert DeNiro
Favorite Movie: Cape Fear • Favorite Color: Red • Favorite Author: Stormie O'Martian
Favorite Car: Nine Three Convertible Saab • Favorite Designer: Gucci
Favorite Make-up Line: MAC • Favorite Sound: Waves crashing on the shore
Favorite Word: "Yes" said really sarcastically • Least Favorite Word: "Shut-up"
Favorite Euphamism: "That's nice" (read: NOT)
Hopes to hear God say when she gets to heaven: Well done my good and faithful servant!

Greatest Hope: That I make it to heaven with lots of jewels in my crown.

Pet Peeve: When Teddy says, "I don't want to hear it." Favorite Profession (barring current one): Music teacher • Least Favorite Profession: Custodian • Greatest Joy: Being a good wife to my husband and a good daughter for my parents • Greatest Heartbreak: My husband's and parents disappointment in me when I've let them down • Find confusing: The differences between men and women • Causes Great Anxiety: Having to go to the airport • Greatest Fear: Not being able to make a positive impact on everyone in my life Thing that most people would be surprised to know about her: That I am one of the most self-conscious people in the world and my own biggest critic

The Ministers

CHAPTER FOUR

Erica

The interesting thing about being a gospel music artist is that there is no separation between career and calling. Your paycheck comes as a byproduct of your ministry. I'm sure it's the same for Christians in many other areas of life. If God has called you to be, say, a book publisher, like the married couple who put out this, our first book, then your ministry is the same as your "job." You have an obligation to make sure that it meets God's standards. It makes no difference if you're a doctor, a student, an attorney, a pastor, a teacher, a used car salesman, a custodian, a football player or an airline pilot. Wherever God has called you, you have an assignment, part of which is to be his representative to the world. You are a holy ambassador for the kingdom of God. So your life better be right. Your attitude better be holy. Your behavior better be godly or you are representing him wrong. Have you ever worked with somebody who claimed to be a Christian, but they cursed worse than a sailor? Or got served by someone wearing a cross around their neck, but they were so mean? How about this, have you ever been given the finger in traffic by somebody who had a fish (a symbol for a Christian) on the back of their car? That's a trip, huh? The thing that we as Christians must remember, no matter where we are, or what we are doing, is that it's possible that we are the only bible some people will ever read. We must live knowing that the Jesus in us is the only Jesus some folks will ever come in contact with. And we must behave accordingly. Now that's not to say that you have to be fake. Somebody asks you how you're doing and you always have to respond "Oh praise the Lord, I'm blessed in Jesus name!" That's not what I'm saying. I'm saying that you should live your life as though the Holy Spirit is alive in you. That's not to say that you won't have struggles or weaknesses. But how you handle those weaknesses and struggles in front of the unsaved people or even the other Christians around you will dictate how effective you are at spreading the Gospel of Jesus Christ. In other words, it will determine your legacy.

This is something that has always been close to my heart. Even as a child, I used to wonder what people would say about me after I was gone. I wondered what kind of mark I would leave and how the world would be different because I had lived. I know, I was a deep little kid. But I did think about these things. They often came up because early in life I began to notice a type of imbalance in the church. I wondered why it was that so many Christians could really love God and be committed to living right, yet, like us, they were so poor. How could someone be a spiritual giant, yet remain a financial midget? Sometimes it seemed that in order to be a good Christian, you almost had to be poor. I knew that couldn't be true, though, because God has infinite resources and he wants us to share in his gifts. He loves us and wants to give us every good thing. But the question still nagged me. Why were so many Christians living defeated, unsuccessful lives? I know that everyone has problems. But if Jesus said that he came to give abundant life, then why were so many of His people just getting by? I was determined to find out why. As I got older, I also became determined that I would experience abundant life. I made up my mind that I couldn't just settle for half an existence when God's word promised me "exceeding, abundantly far above all I could ever ask or think."

I'm still seeking God on why so many of his people live below his standard. He has given me some revelation. If you talk to lots of people, you learn quickly that they hate their jobs. That's a big problem, too, when you consider that most people spend more waking hours at work than they do at home. I don't mean to get too deep, or anything, but I think lots of Christians pursue jobs or careers in order to make money instead of because God called them. Some people even ignore God's call because they don't see how they could support themselves or what future they could possibly have in a given profession. And I don't just mean the call to preach. I mean that God could have called you to be an actor, but because you didn't see how you could be successful right away, or because somebody told you that you needed to look for a "real" job, you ignored God. God could have called you to go to college, but since you couldn't figure out how to pay for it, or you didn't have the grades, you gave up.

I am convinced that our joy lies in following God's will for our lives. Think about it, if God is who He said He is, meaning, He created the universe and everything and everyone in it, then wouldn't he know his plans for you? He parted the Red Sea, but he can't get you into college? He hung every star in the heavens and has numbered every hair on your head, but He doesn't know that you need a car? I don't think so. God has a perfect, unique plan for each one of us and he wants us to live it out. The best thing is that whatever it is, it's better than anything we could ever imagine for ourselves. But you have to do your part. You've got to ask him what he wants you to do. Then you've got to go after it with all your heart. When I was a little girl, singing in the choir at Evangelistic C.O.G.I.C., I could never have guessed that God would lead me to become a platinum selling recording artist. I just wanted to sing. I encourage you to ask God what he wants you to do. Even if you think you already know. Ask him until he tells you. Keep your spiritual eyes and ears open for his answer. Then hold on! You'll be in for the ride of your life! He's faithful. I promise you, He won't let you down!

Tina and I are definitely operating in our calling. And it is wonderful. I am so grateful to God for my career! Sometimes I can't believe that I get paid to sing! I mean, I would sing for free! And for a long time I did! It has been an incredible journey so far. I'm sure that it will only get more and more exciting. We try really hard to make sure that we represent God well in everything we do. This affects everything from how we talk, to how we dress, to where we will perform. Our mission is very clear and simple. We bring the message of the Gospel to the world. We're in an interesting position. Because our look and our music is so contemporary and youthful, our lyrics reach people who might not ever open a bible. People attend our concerts who might not ever go to church. That's why we take every opportunity to talk about how good God is. We don't clobber people over the head or anything. We don't scream at people that if they don't get saved then they're going to hell. That's not our style. We simply tell people in song and in testimony about how good God is and has been to us. Then we invite them to get to know him. We don't pressure anybody. There's no alter call or anything like that. We stress that the decision to walk with God is a personal one. One that only the individual can make. And it can be made anywhere. You don't have to come to church to get saved. You could be in your car, in your bedroom, at work, in the bathroom. God is everywhere, so wherever you are is good enough. We emphasize that God is always ready to receive any person who wants to have a relationship with him any time. That's part of the significance behind the name Mary Mary. The "Mary's" were two women at opposite ends of the spiritual spectrum. There was Mary, the mother of Jesus. God chose her because of her purity (she was a virgin), and because of her willingness to serve the kingdom. She told Gabriel "Let it be done unto me according to your word." She is an excellent example of what a woman should be. Then there was Mary Magdeline, a prostitute (until she met Jesus). In Jewish society, she was considered the lowest of the low. She had no value and no worth in the eyes of the religious leaders of her day. She was the antithesis of virtue. But Jesus embraced her, too. His love changed her life! The two Mary's were very different, but Jesus loved and honored them both. It just goes to show, God stands willing to accept you no matter what your station in life, no matter what you've done, no matter good or how bad you've been. He loves us all. He wants to have a personal, real, intimate relationship with each of us.

Because Tina and I minister God's word wherever we go, it's real important that we stay connected to him through prayer, fellowship and studying the Holy Bible. We are very busy, but we can't afford to neglect our time with him. When we're on the road, it's hard to go to church services consistently. But we still worship and pray. When we're at home in Southern, CA Tina and her husband, my brother-in-law, Teddy Campbell, attend the church where we grew up, Evangelistic C.O.G.I.C.. My husband, Warryn Campbell and I attend West Angeles. We love God and we love spending time with our respective church families. But beyond wanting to be with God, we must spend time with him whether we "feel" up to it or not. Otherwise, we'll find ourselves ministering the gospel of Tina and Erica instead of the Gospel of Jesus Christ. And the last time I checked, nobody got saved that way. And if nobody is getting saved, if lives aren't being changed, if people aren't making decisions for Christ, then even if we sell hundreds of millions of albums the world over, we've failed.

My personal routine has to be flexible because of my schedule. But I try to be as consistent as possible. On average, I have quiet time for at least two hours everyday. During that time alone with God, I study the bible. I worship and meditate. I don't have a structured routine, just whatever feels right from day to day. Mostly though I try to live a life of worship. I don't do drugs. I am a faithful, loving, submitted wife to my husband. I honor my parents. I could list a lot of things that I don't do, but suffice it to say that if it's not glorifying to God, then I try not to do it. Like everyone else, I have good days and bad days. Some days I feel like I'm on top of my game, because everything is going well. Other times, I feel like, "You are such a loser! Pull it together!" Not every day is a great one. But that's part of life. That's how it works. It's a process and we have to stay dependent on God for every single thing.

Back when we were having difficulty with our sophomore project, we realized part of why we got so far off track was because we had not been seeking God as diligently as we should have been. Tina said that she had been getting into bed saying no more than a customary prayer we used to say as children. For us, the habit of saying this prayer was the same as saying "God bless you,"

My pastor used to say that we
didn't have to try to change the way people
dress when they came to church.
He'd say just fill them up with enough of
the Holy Ghost and they'll change on
their own. The Holy Spirit convicts
people, not other people.

to someone who had sneezed. It wasn't deep; it didn't require quieting your spirit and inviting in the Holy Spirit. It was like an afterthought. I had been guilty of that, too, taking God for granted because things had been going so well. We had been so busy working for God that we had forgotten that we worked for God. Do you know what I mean? We had gotten so caught up in doing kingdom work that we neglected the King!

Tina says that another part of our problem is that we had gotten spoiled. I agree with her. We grew up in church. We had good word poured into us at least two or three times a week. We got fed at Sunday morning services, Wednesday night bible study and Thursday night youth services. We didn't have to work really hard to study the word because it was always being delivered to us so well and so frequently. When we got on our own, we pretty much kept up the same poor habits that we had had at home. Pretty soon we experienced not only the attacks on our careers and on our family, but personally as well. We suddenly seemed ineffective. We wondered if we were reaching people. Even though it had only been a few years, we wondered if we were stale. Trying to bring the word in our own strength, we fell flat on our faces. So guess what? We began to study, have quiet time alone with God, to pray and worship more often. We hadn't really taken into consideration the ministry aspect of our career when we first started. We just wanted to sing to the Lord. We knew how hard ministry was, just by watching the members of our family, who were preachers and what have you. We knew the risk of opening yourself up to attacks from the enemy because you're damaging his kingdom. We certainly knew that. We just didn't think we'd merit that much attention from the enemy. Now that we understand how much bigger than us, this is, we make time to equip ourselves. We have a responsibility to our fans to bring fresh word. We have a responsibility to God to study, so that we can be "ready in and out of season."

Our dilemma happens a lot in churches and in the lives of individuals, too. Sometimes we Christians are so busy acting like Martha, preparing the dinner, cleaning the house, getting ready for this conference, praying with this person, ministering in this situation, witnessing in that situation, that we forget to sit at Jesus' feet, like Mary did, and just be close. When we don't make time to be close to Jesus, we can suffer severe burnout. Chaos follows because things that we could have known about, or gotten a handle on had we been listening to the Holy Spirit, blow up in our faces and catches us off guard. Not to mention it's just good to be close to God...not asking him for anything, not wanting anything, just being quiet in his presence. When I was a little girl, sometimes I would just sit on my Daddy's lap, I wouldn't talk or anything. I'd just sit there. I've seen little kids in the grocery store or at church sometimes, just hugging their mother's leg. They aren't talking. They aren't even looking at her. They're just holding on, just being close. If we have enough sense to do that as children, we should certainly have enough sense to do that as adults with our Heavenly Father. We should just hang out sometimes, sit on Daddy's lap and just let him hold us.

When I take time to do this, I am a better minister, singer, sister, friend, wife, daughter. Seeking God's face has helped Tina and me a great deal in dealing with our critics. Without giving them too much attention here, there are people who reject us specifically because we aren't traditional

People have
expressed concern
about how Tina and
I dress because
we don't wear
what I like to call
"Saved gear."

Our hair isn't
pulled back in
a bun; we're not
sportin' a long
skirt, a turtle
neck, stockings and
sensible pumps.

gospel artists. If we had not been convinced of our calling, their jabs at us could have really shaken our confidence early on. Because we have such a close relationship with the Lord, we are able to handle our critics in love. We are not the first generation of non-traditional gospel singers. The Winans, Tremaine Hawkins, The Mighty Clouds of Joy, Kirk Franklin and many others came before us. And all of those performers caught flack because of their unique styles. If Jesus' life is any indicator, the fact that we are criticized is a sign to us that we were on the right track. Jesus had a bunch of critics. The religious leaders of his day were very disturbed by his apparent lack of respect for tradition. He was greatly persecuted for not following the norm. Not to say that we are Jesus. But we do follow him. And whenever you do that, you can bet the devil is not going to be happy and he's going to be very vocal about it, too. Our ministry walks us right into the enemy's territory. God uses us to lead the lost to him. He uses our message to spread hope and joy to a very sorrowful world. Of course the enemy is going to attack us. We don't welcome it, but we do expect it. Seeking God's ways just makes us better able to treat our critics with love and respect.

Ironically, mainstream people have only nice things to say about us. Our biggest criticism comes from our own...saved folks in the church. Isn't that something? I understand that when the mission is different from what people are used to, they don't get it, so they judge it. Still I think that the brethren should be careful when they criticize God's man or woman. God gives the vision to whomever he sees fit. You probably wouldn't do the Mary Mary thing the same way Tina and Erica do. But He didn't give our assignment to you. In the same way, we wouldn't necessarily do your thing the same way you do it. But again, that's your assignment, not ours. He uses us all to reach different parts of the world with his message, and he does so with purpose. We Christians could all stand to apply Romans 14 to our varied opinions and practices. Oddly enough, some of my favorite traditional gospel artists, legends, like Pastor Shirley Caesar, Mom and Pop Winans, Hezekiah Walker and Dr. Bobby Jones have personally encouraged us to continue on the road that we're on. It's humbling to hear that a great gospel figure, whom you've respected and listened to your whole life, not only knows your music, but is a fan! That still trips me out.

People have expressed concern about how Tina and I dress because we don't wear what I like to call "saved gear." Our hair isn't pulled back in a bun; we're not sportin' a long skirt, a turtle neck, stockings and sensible pumps. And again even though we don't look traditional, we are so very conservative. I agree that many secular artists today show a little too much sometimes. I don't believe that if you have talent that you have to use sex to sell your music. Besides, what happens once your body goes? If it's all about your breasts or your bare midriff, then who's listening to your lyrics? Who respects your music or your talent? Of course, if you are a Christian artist, then skimpy, revealing clothes aren't even an option. You represent God and he's real clear about modesty. Your image can't contradict his message. The only person who needs to see me dressed sexy is my husband. Besides, it's not like the only other option is a potato sack dress or unkempt, nappy hair. We do highlight our femininity. After all, we are women, God's women. And one thing my mom and my aunt always tell us, "You make sure you look cute!" Being saved and modest can also be appealing. I want to feel pretty and to look good. It's not like only ugly people serve the Lord. God wants our best.

I love to wear just
about anything by
Juicy, DKNY,
Nike, and Dolce
and Gabanna. I
really like the way
Roberto Covalli's
jeans fit. I
also like vintage
clothing. Mary
Mary's style is
contemporary but
conservative,
stylish yet
modest.

There are a whole lot of people who don't go to church on Sundays. They wash their cars or go to ball games. To them Christmas has nothing to do with Jesus and neither does Easter. Our job is to introduce Christ to those people. And we can't come looking and acting intimidating. They have to see some similarities. They have to recognize that we have something in common that makes them feel like they can talk to us. We write songs that people, who don't necessarily go to church, can relate to. Maybe they were wounded by the church or had a bad experience that drew them away. Our mission, Mary Mary's mission is to teach people who God is. We're not interested in all the "isms," the "schisms" or any of that other divisive stuff. We just want people to learn about him. There's so much division in the body of Christ already. There are so many denominations, and then even in-fighting within denominations, because we've all got our big ol' opinions up in the way. We're so busy passing judgment on each other that we forget about the world! I've heard Christians say things like, "Well my church, we definitely are going to heaven. We'll be in the V.I.P. seats. Y'all church will have the cheap seats." But the last time I checked, there was no mention of V.I.P. seating in heaven. All that competition is foolishness. Jesus prayed for the body to be one. So Mary Mary just tries to give people God.

My pastor used to say that we didn't have to try to change the way people dress when they came to church. He'd say just fill them up with enough of the Holy Ghost and they'll change on their own. The Holy Spirit convicts people, not other people. The bible says "with loving kindness have I drawn you." There was this one time I dressed inappropriately for church. This one older lady approached me to discuss it. Her manner was so gentle that I never forgot what she said to me. She said, "You're a beautiful girl and that's a beautiful dress. I think it's perfect for a cocktail party or for a dance. But it is just a little too short for church. But it is really cute and you do look good in it." The way she said it was so sweet and so loving, that I agreed with her and left smiling! I accepted her gentle correction joyously! Can you imagine if everyone in the body treated everyone else in the body like that? We're more likely to say something like, "Now girl, you know that dress is too short and too tight to be wearing to church!" Not to say that there aren't times when you need to come strong. Sometimes that is necessary, but even a harsh rebuke needs to be delivered in the spirit of love, not in pride or arrogance. Pride and arrogance say, "I'm better than you. You need to do it this way, not that way. I'm right and you're wrong." If we come to a person in humility, lovingly suggesting a change, they're bound to be more receptive to what we have to say.

The love and humility of Christ is what Tina and I try to convey in our music. So many people think that just because they live a less than perfect life, that they can't approach God. But that's not true. We share that we're just regular folks and God loves us. So – he loves you, too. And that's not just Erica and Tina's job, that's every Christian's job. As a whole we could stand to show a lot more of Christ's love to the world. People live with enough judgment. The world is already a rough, mean place. People don't need the Church, perpetually shaking a finger in their faces. They need to know that God is not some mean, pushy, judgmental ogre, who's waiting to zap you with a lighting rod, but a kind, gentle and loving father, who stands ready to hug you. As you get closer to Him, He will tell you about yourself, but in such a way that you will start to examine your behavior. He'll have you talking to yourself, "Why do I keep doing that?" or "You know that isn't working for me. Maybe I should stop," or "I don't feel good about myself when I do that." But in order for a person to be in the position to examine his or her life, (s)he's got to meet Him first.

So all of that to say, that's why we dress the way we do. Tina is more of a Gucci fan. I love to wear just about anything by Juicy, DKNY, Nike, and Dolce and Gabanna. I really like the way Roberto Covalli's jeans fit. I also like vintage clothing. Mary Mary's style is contemporary but conservative, stylish yet modest. Where the spirit of the Lord is, there is freedom. We wear pretty much anything we like as long as it's tasteful and shows no flesh. We have too much respect for God, our parents, our husbands and ourselves to wear anything that would compromise God's message.

My advice to artists who are just starting out is to be true to yourself. Sex definitely sells, but do you want it to sell you? Don't be vampish, just because you think the public or executives expect it. Be a cut above the ordinary. Be original, not common. Be timeless. Even if you are pursuing a career in secular music, you don't have to be naked to sell an album. For every skinny, naked girl, there's a tasteful young woman with real talent. Some of my favorite artists include Jill Scott, India Irie, Yolanda Adams, Cece Winans, Dorinda Clark-Cole, and Alicia Keys. None of those women sing naked; neither should you.

You should try to be your best self. And you should be true to your vision. If your best self is a size 16, then be a size 16 and be proud! By the same token, if your best self is a size 5, then don't settle for a size 12. Only you can say what feels authentic. Do not prostitute yourself for the sake of record sales. Don't commit to a false, slutty image only to have to come back in a couple of years and reinvent yourself when you have more control over your project. If you come out as your best self, you automatically give your marketing execs something to work with. You just make sure that your image does not contradict your message, especially if you sing gospel.

As entertainers, whether our field is music, acting or sports we have a responsibility for how we present ourselves to the public. We are responsible because the choices we make as individuals affect the public at large. To whom much is given, much is required. Life in the spotlight is challenging because people get to know things about your personal life that they would never know if you weren't a celebrity. Famous people can often be the target of unfair publicity and nuisance lawsuits. And tabloids will print lies. And people, even your most loyal fans, will gobble them up. It's not fair. But life is not fair. That's part of the trade off we make. We get to be famous and people get to know about us. For this reason, I don't believe that people who make their living by being in the public eye have a right to say that they are not role models. Although I understand why they make the claim. We are role models by default, whether we want to be or not. Our choices influence the choices of many other people. That's what it means to be a role model. It's an awesome responsibility when you think about it. Having the ability to influence people's choices. Designers and other manufacturers know that celebrities have tremendous influence. That's why they give them so much free stuff. Their hope is that if fans see their favorite stars rockin' a certain purse, shoe, dress or suit, then those same fans will run out and buy those exact same items. Male and female alike copy celebrity trends.

Just as fans of all ages emulate their idols' clothing and gadgets, they emulate their thinking and lifestyles, too. Youths and young adults are particularly vulnerable. That's why special interest groups like P.E.T.A. and Amnesty International and corporations like Wells Fargo and Sprint use celebrity spokespersons to advance their causes and to push their goods. They already know that famous people influence the way the world thinks. So if a celebrity can make the world a better place for animals and prisoners of war, shouldn't that carry over into a concern for our youth? If as a celebrity, you dress provocatively, and make it look glamorous, or make it seem like it's cool to sleep with hordes of people, you bare some responsibility for the millions of teenagers and young people who try to dress and act just like you. The same goes if you teach a message of hope, peace, love and self-respect. At the heart of Mary Mary is an acute awareness of just how much we can affect change in the world through Christ. That is our calling. That is our mission.

Tina

As far as the role model thing goes, your first role models should come from home. Parents also need to take responsibility for setting a good example for their own children to follow instead of just relying on examples from the media. But the real problem is a much greater one. America needs to put God back into our society. His presence would make a world of difference. We need to put prayer back in schools. We've made it almost a sin to even mention the name of Jesus in public. Americans are allowed to talk about anything else, homosexuality, heterosexuality, drugs, pornography, and whatever else comes to mind. But mention the name of Jesus Christ at school? In the work place? Everybody wants to beat you over the head. On talk shows, you can talk about all other world religions. You can even talk about what your psychic or your astrologer told you. But quote the bible? Oh, it's all over. You get shut down by the host! If we invite Jesus Christ back into our society at large, a lot of the craziness that we have to protect our kids from, will calm down. The fear of God will keep a person, even a role model, from doing a whole bunch of foolishness.

I am on a mission for the Lord, no doubt. But I do want to have fun! It's fun to be able to sing with my sister on stage! It's fun to meet lots of enthusiastic fans. It's incredible to go on tour with a great artist, like Kirk Franklin. It's cool to be able to record a song that I wrote and to hear it playing on the radio. It's exciting to be able to walk into 100.3 The Beat in Los Angeles and spend the morning laughing and talking with Steve Harvey. And it's really great to get free stuff. And yes, it's fun to make a lot of money doing something that I love to do! I won't lie. I am having a great time doing this singing thing for God. We want people to know that life in Christ can be exciting and deeply fulfilling. This is what abundant life is all about. When you are doing what God has called you to do and you are depending upon him to make it happen? You are in the best posi-

My advice to
artists who
are just starting
out is to be
true to yourself...

Don't be vampish,
just because
you think the
public or
executives
expect it.

tion possible. It can be scary, but at the same time, it can be wonderful. You have joy, so even if you go through a rough time, first of all, you know that at some point it will end. And you don't have to wait until it ends to celebrate, you can celebrate now! As a matter of fact, you should keep celebrating until something changes and then you can celebrate some more!

The thing that's so great about God is that he often gives you the desire before he calls you. Erica and I have been singing practically our whole lives! We have always loved music and performing, specifically singing for and to God. Like Erica said, we did it for free for a long time before it ever occurred to us that we could get paid for it. See? And God is like that. I think some people are afraid to ask him what he wants them to do because they think he's going to put them on a missionary field somewhere in the middle of Africa. And you know what? He could do that since he's in charge. But he could also lead you into medicine, politics, sports, the arts. Who knows? Our nation's national security advisor, Condoleezza Rice had considered becoming a music teacher, once she realized that she didn't possess the talent to become a concert pianist. However, when she discovered her true calling – a major in international politics with a concentration in Soviet studies, while attending the University of Denver, she said the feeling was "like falling in love." She just knew suddenly that that's what she wanted to do. Obviously her choice was the correct one. In her obedience God has taken her many places and her major has served her very well everywhere, including in her current position. So you see, God's got a great plan for your life. You never know where you'll end up. But you've got to do your part and move forward. After all there wouldn't have been any need for God to part the Red Sea if the Israelites had never left Egypt.

Take a chance on God! See where he leads you. Of course following him into new territory will require more of you. You will have to stay in the word. But believe it or not, it won't be a burden. You'll develop a hunger to know God's word because it contains the key to your destiny. And he will meet you right where you are. It's amazing to me how when Erica and I study a certain passage in scripture, if we need some insight, or a more thorough explanation of what we've read, no matter how long we've been on the road, whenever we do get a chance to attend church, the pastor, in whatever city we're in will be teaching from that same passage, sometimes down to the exact same verse! It floors me every time. But God is like that. Because He meets you and wets your appetite, you'll find that you want to pray more fervently and more often. You'll want to continually live in his presence. Once you experience the closeness of God in a relationship where he's walking hand in hand with you, leading you from glory to glory to glory, you won't want to let anything or anyone come between you and Him. Like I said, give it a try. Take a risk. Enjoy the journey!

FOOD FOR THOUGHT

Read 1 Corinthians 12:1-11

1. God equips every person with at least one gift. What are your gifts?

2. How are you putting them to use?

_____
_____
_____
_____
_____
_____
_____
_____
_____
_____
_____

3. What have you done to cultivate them?

_____
_____
_____
_____
_____
_____
_____
_____
_____
_____

_____

_____

_____

_____

_____

_____

_____

_____

_____

_____

_____

_____

4. Do this: Ask God to show your gifts to you. Ask him how he wants you to use them to make the world a better place.

_____

_____

_____

_____

_____

_____

_____

_____

_____

_____

Thomasina Andrea Atkins
aka "Goo Goo," our sister.
She got her nickname from my cousin,
Dana, who came to live with us
around the same time "Goo Goo"
was born. He started calling
her that and it just stuck.

The Family

CHAPTER FIVE

Tina

The Atkins' clan is a gi-normous one. Our immediate birth family consists of eleven people. We'd like you to meet them. They are:

Eddie A. Atkins, Jr., our father. He was born and raised in Merced, California. His family was what's now considered the working poor. He has one sister, Aunt Lavera, and lots of other relatives. His parents are the late Eddie A. Atkins, Senior and Levada Cruthird. Our dad was raised in church and really knows the bible. He spent time in the military, which accounts for his obsession with order. When we were little, he ran our home somewhat like a nursery school boot camp. Everything had a place. Everyone had a duty. He called our kitchen the mess hall and our bathroom the latrene. On some mornings, when he didn't have to go to work, he would come into our rooms, banging on the back of a pot to wake us up. We'd be grumpy and annoyed. But on those occasions, he always had the best pancake breakfast waiting for us at the table! Our dad still makes the world's best pancakes! He's really crazy, always ready to laugh or tell a story. He is, however, quite the perfectionist. If it's not right, don't bother. I'm a lot like him.

Thomasina Atkins, our mother.
She was born in Stamford, Connecticut to Tommy and Ruth Daniels. My grandmother made a good living as a housekeeper. My mom was kind of a "girlie" girl. She stayed well groomed and was always well mannered. She's the baby in her family. She has four sisters. She has always been easy-going and quiet. She loves the Lord and has always lived upright in front of us. She has always been somewhat of a stickler for etiquette and discipline. She raised us all to be young ladies, to take good care of ourselves and to look cute. She taught us more eternal values as well. But we were never to underestimate the importance of being polite and neat.

Darrell Antoine Atkins, our oldest brother.
Since sixteen, he has dubbed himself, the first, the only the original. He has a tough exterior, but inside, he's a big softie. As children, he always protected us from bullies. Many a-would-be-fight was stopped in its tracks by the words: "I'm going to tell my brother on you!" At home, though, it was a different story. He was a tyrant! People always felt sorry for him because he had so many sisters. But we needed the pity. We were pretty much his slaves! He'd have us bringing him his sandwiches and drinks. He totally monopolized the T.V. We'd be begging to watch cartoons, while he sat propped up in front of the screen watching some western. I think I hate westerns for that reason, even now. He has always been really smart and done well in school. Apart from the tyranny, he was usually very well mannered. All of the mothers at church used to comment on how nice "Thomasina's boy" was. He did a stint in one of the local gangs. I think he was most impressed with the sense of family and male companionship that gang life offered. When he got older, he turned in his membership and moved to Arizona. He lives there now with two of his children.

Maliea Dionne Atkins, our sister.

She's also a big ol' softie, but without the hard exterior. She's a natural organizer and extremely family oriented. Erica really looked up to her when she was younger. When Erica was in junior high and Maliea was in senior high, Erica coveted this red Guess sweatshirt that Maliea always wore. When Erica got that thing as a hand-me-down, she wore it out! Erica was so close to Maliea that Maliea's boyfriends often called her their "little girlfriend." What Erica didn't know was that they were just being nice to her. One day she followed Maliea and her boyfriend at the time, Richard, when they left church. When she caught up to them, they were kissing! Erica was totally devastated. She was only twelve at the time and could not figure out why her "boyfriend" was kissing her sister! To this day, we still tease her about that. I admire Maliea, too. To me she is a wonderful single mom. She has raised her two sons, Jay and Travon very well. They respect her highly and love her immensely. They can talk to her about anything and are very open with her. I'm going to study her methods once I become a mom.

Andre Lavelle Atkins, our brother.

Although he was older Erica and I were, we always thought of him as our little brother because he was always so small. He was born with Down's syndrome, spinal meningitis and a hole in his heart. The doctors told my parents that he wouldn't live past four years old. But he lived until he was six. And even though he spent more than sixty-five percent of his short life in the hospital, my parents were always grateful that he had been born into our family. They never said things like "Why us, God?" They just loved our brother and thanked God for every day that they got to spend with him. And because of their example, we did the same. Our brother was really weak and frail. But when his health allowed us to, Erica and I would play with him. I remember one time my mom was in another part of the house. And when she came back, Erica, Andre, and I were on top of the refrigerator! For the life of me, I don't remember how we got up there. I just remember the look on my mom's face when she found us. I don't remember if we got in trouble or not; we were so young. But that just goes to show that we didn't think of him as "poor Andre" who was sick. To us he was just our brother. We saw him that way because that's how our parents saw him. He was just one more member of the Atkins' clan.

My parents' joy over Andre's life didn't meant that they weren't concerned about his condition or that they pretended it didn't exist. In fact it was just the opposite. They prayed for him (and all of us, really) and taught us to do the same. They used his life as an opportunity to show us just how awesome God is. My father would constantly remind us that God often uses adversity to build character in His children. He took every opportunity to tell us that because God wants us to be like Jesus, He lets us go through hard times and difficult tests to make sure that we conform to Christ's image. So then no struggle is just for the heck of it. Pain and suffering always have a purpose.

Because of having had Andre in my life, I have a special place in my heart for the developmentally disabled. Every time I see someone, especially a child, who has Down Syndrome or some other mental disability, I'm just filled with God's love for that person. I just want to run up to them and hug them. I usually don't because most times it would be inappropriate. But the experience usually makes me remember Andre and how special he was to me. When he died, I remember most how it affected my father. I remember looking at Andre's little, tiny coffin and understanding that he was gone. I wept. I remember some adult saying that I didn't really know what was happening. But they were wrong. I understood perfectly.

Erica Monique Atkins Campbell, the only planned pregnancy in our family.

Trecina Evette Atkins Campbell aka "Tina"

Delisa Marie Atkins Brown aka "Lisa" or "Wittle Wees," our sister.
She has known since she was five years old that she wanted to be a doctor. She is a very focused and determined young woman. Once she makes up her mind to do a thing, it's done. When she graduated from high school, she went to Concordia University in Wisconsin and knocked out her B.A. in four years flat. She's now continuing her studies to become an herbalist, here in Southern California. Currently she is studying Chinese medicine. She's the first in our family to graduate from a four-year college. Needless to say, we are very proud of her. She got married to a wonderful guy, named Erroll Brown in April of 2002. He's studying medicine, too. They are a perfect match. Her goal is to open her own private practice one day, specializing in holistic medicine and healing. Lisa's demeanor is real laid back. She will listen to your opinions about her choices, but in the end, she is going to do, what she has decided. Beneath her low key, sarcastic sense of humor, beats the heart of a very caring young woman.

Thomasina Andrea Atkins aka "Goo Goo,"our sister.
She got her nickname from my cousin, Dana, who came to live with us around the same time "Goo Goo" was born. He started calling her that and it just stuck. She is the comedienne of the family and my laughing partner. She was and always has been really funny. We used to call her "the poet" when she was younger, because she'd write these funny, quirky requests in the form of a poem. If she needed a favor, like a ride to the mall or to borrow something, instead of asking, she'd write a poem and give it to us. Oddly enough she parlayed that into writing music. She's very talented. Her songs are really good. She sings background for Mary Mary, but that's beneath her talent. Because she has such a big personality, Erica thinks her calling may be on the stage, or on the screen. Even though she is now a young adult, she still considers herself the baby of the family, despite the fact that we have two sisters younger than she is. I must admit, we all treat Goo Goo like she's the baby. Maybe that's why she won't give up the position.

Alana Ellesse Atkins aka "Lainz" or "Luv Luv"
When Alana was a little girl, all she wanted to do was to give everyone hugs and kisses. She started singing solos when she was three. She has also sung background for Mary Mary. She has a beautiful voice, but no desire to use it professionally. Her long term goal is to become a veteri-

Like Tina, I give glory
to God for making my
parents wise
in the way that they
raised us.

They always expected
the best behavior out
of us kids. They
didn't always get it,
but they held up a
standard anyway.

narian. Her short term goal is to join the army. We have all tried to talk her out of it. But her response is always the same: "Thank you, but I still want to go." She's really mature and very focused. Like Lisa, once Alana has decided to pursue something, it's as good as done. She has taken on the role of the "older sister" at home now. The last batch of teens at the house, which include my youngest sister, Shanta, and Darrell's two older daughters, Jazzmine and Deshane, all look to Alana for guidance and advice. She's one of the most sophisticated teenagers I know. She's really got her act together. Along with my nieces mentioned above and my sister's sons, Jay and Travon, we affectionately refer to them collectively as "The Rat Pack."

Shanta Nena Lave Atkins, our baby sister.

She is the genius entrepreneur in the making. She's going to make the whole family proud and extremely rich. We'll be millionaires for decades to come off her efforts. She sells whatever she can get her hands on. Mostly she buys candy wholesale, then sells it retail. Her attitude is that since she's not old enough to get a job permit, and she needs to make money, she's just got to be creative. And she's making a killing, too. Everywhere she goes, she carries two back-packs. One holds her books, the other, a ton of candy. She accounts for every penny, too. If she's missing thirty-five cents, she knows exactly where it went. At first we didn't really take her little enterprise that seriously. But about two years ago, she bought everybody in the family gifts. We were expecting little trinkets or something like that. But she came with it! She bought us all really nice department store gifts! She gave us items, like designer shoes, stylish shirts, and purses. They were really nice! The entire family was flabbergasted. We wondered how she could afford such expensive stuff. She told us that she bought it out of her earnings from candy sales. She had a nice little cache set aside in a bank account. Needless to say, we took her business seriously from that point on.

Erica and I are both married to men whose last names are Campbell although their families are not related. My husband is Teddy Campbell. He's a sincere, loving man. He's a dedicated, hard work-er and a great provider. He's considerate of and concerned about me. He loves the Lord. He's fun-loving, full of energy, and just a little crazy. He doesn't have a tough-as-nails exterior, but it does take some doing to pull the sensitive side out of him. He was born and raised in Chicago, Ill.

When I married, I not only got a great husband but a bunch of really wonderful in-laws, too. My husband's family consists of his mom, Louise Campbell, his aunt Carolyn Campbell, his cousin (Carolyn's son), Marcus Campbell, Aunt Cathy and Uncle Bob Wooten, Auntie Reen and Uncle Fred, and their daughter, Joy Campbell.

I'll let Erica tell you about her own husband and his family.

performing

backstage

Chillin'

rollin' to the venue

Erica

My husband's name is Warryn Campbell. As stated in a previous chapter, we met while Tina and I were on tour with "Mama I'm Sorry" and he was playing for Brandy. Warryn is sweet, funny, outgoing, but quiet when you first meet him. He's respectable and respectful. He's my best friend, my buddy, my "dog." He was born and raised in Watts, California. He attended both Hamilton and Westchester High Schools. His mom and dad didn't have a whole lot, but they worked hard to provide a loving home environment for their children. Warryn is driven and knows exactly what he wants. When he graduated from high school, he opted not to go to college so that he could pursue a career in music. He has a beautiful voice, as does his sister Joi Campbell. He sings background vocals on a few Mary Mary songs, but he never tells anyone! My wonderful in-laws include Warryn's parents, Warryn and Sandra Campbell and his sister, Joi. Joi is extremely gifted and can sing her butt off! She puts together many of the ensembles that Tina and I wear on stage and off. She has recently signed a recording contract with J records and will be coming out with her own album very soon! That's it, that's the Atkins/Campbell clan! We've got a gang of other relatives and extended family. Space does not permit us to list all of their names, but we love them all!

If I've said it once, I'll say it a thousand times. Family is what we are all about. Tina and I cherish our close relationships with our mother and father, brothers and sisters, husbands and in-laws. God had really blessed us with a wealth of wonderful, good-hearted people, who love him. It has made all the difference in our lives, in our careers and in our relationship with the Lord. When I think about the fact that so many families are divided or torn apart by divorce or in-fighting, I thank God for preserving us. I'm sure that growing up poor had a lot to do with why we're all so close. When you go through difficult times together as a family, they can really cement your bonds.

Like Tina, I give glory to God for making my parents wise in the way that they raised us. They always expected the best behavior out of us kids. They didn't always get it, but they held up a standard anyway. One thing that they never waffled on was discipline. One thing that always guaranteed a spanking was fighting with one another. Whenever we fought, we got spanked, no exceptions. Afterwards we always had to apologize, make up and hug. We hated hugging. But eventually we also got sick of fighting. I'm not saying that we don't still have our disagreements. We are not some perfect portrait of a family where everyone smiles and greets each other with "Why hello dear sister how are you this fine morning?" We're not cheesy or fake like that. We argue. And we can get loud, too. Real loud. But whatever we disagree about, the spat always ends in laughter. Somebody will tell a joke and everybody will bust up laughing. Schisms aren't allowed in our family. We try to get resolved by bedtime, too. Our parents never allowed us to stay mad at each other. Stamping out anger is a good way to keep your family close.

Our parents always prayed with us and for us, too. Some of my happiest memories from childhood are of us all gathered around the bed, praying before going to sleep. I guess it's true that a

Our family surrounds us in this business. My husband, Warryn, produces us. Tina's husband, Teddy, oversees our live music for us.

My sister, Thomasina, sings background vocals for us. And as I mentioned, my sister-in-law, Joi Campbell, is our stylist sometimes.

"family that prays together stays together." I know it sounds very bumper-stickery, but it's definitely true in our case. Another key thing that our parents did was to bring us to church, not just send us. A lot of parents think that just because their children come in contact with the church building that that's enough to put them on the right track. Our parents took an active role in our lives, especially where our relationship with God was concerned. They spent time not just reading the word to us, but explaining it, too. They taught us the habits of maintaining a relationship with God long before we understood the importance of doing so.

The most effective thing our parents did for us was to live out their faith in front of our eyes. My mother never complained about our living situation. She didn't sink into depressions. She didn't drown her sorrows with anything. Truthfully, she didn't even speak negatively. She was always really positive and hopeful. She was and continues to be a loving, devoted mother. She lived godly before us. She was always praying! Sometimes we would wake up in the morning with anointing oil on our heads, from her prayers that she sent up while we slept. Sometimes I'd hear her walking the floor at night and praying over us, making her requests known to God. She always made sure that she lived in such a way as to put herself in a position where God could bless her. Morally speaking, she was as upright as they come to us.

I am most impressed with her obedience to the Holy Spirit. She gave birth to nine children! Lots of women in her position would have said, "no more." They would have allowed fear of lack of money or people's criticism's to deter them from having so many kids. But she didn't. Whenever I asked how she could have so many children, she would say, "God said to be fruitful and multiply." I'm also proud of how she handled the criticism of the saints. You know how it is. Folks see eleven of you piling out of a two-door Datsun, they will make comments, some of them not so kind. I know my mother heard what they said, because I did. But she only responded to her critics in love and in faith. I know she sounds amazing. She is! Only as a grown woman can I better appreciate the enormity of her task, especially given all that she went through with my dad's illness and my brother's sickness and subsequent death. I figure if she could handle her stuff with dignity and an unwavering faith in God, I certainly can stop whining about whatever situations I may have to face. You know?

My father sets just as wonderful an example as my mom. He's a military man, so he tends to be somewhat of a perfectionist. He believes that there is a particular way to do everything, whether it's loading the dishwasher, washing the table or folding clothes. Tina is a lot like him. He has always given leadership to our family, while at the same time being very loving and compassionate. Early on in his life, despite his surroundings in Merced, California, or maybe because of them, he made a decision to live for Christ. He was determined that he was not going to engage in the lifestyle that many of the male members of his family embraced. He had seen where it led them and he was not impressed. Because of his decision, he became determined to reach young men for Christ. He ministered to prison inmates. I remember that he wore regular clothes, just jeans, tennis shoes and a shirt, never his clergy collar. He did this purposefully, so the inmates would feel more comfortable approaching him and opening up to him. He talked to all the young men in our neighborhood, too. Because he was so cool with them, they often sought him out. Sometimes they would even confide in him about things they were about to do. They asked for advice on relationships with girls, school, career, parents, you name it. Because of the ministry my father had, I really feel in my heart that's why Tina and I have the type of ministry and style that we do. He wasn't as concerned with looking like he was part of the church as he was with showing the love of Christ. His is an impressive legacy, especially when you consider his roots.

My father constantly taught us that adversity is how God builds character and that just because times get difficult doesn't mean that you can leave or quit. I've talked to him about the severity of the pressures he must have felt, raising nine children, combating a debilitating illness and surviving the death of a child. He maintains that your past does not dictate your future. Regardless of where you come from, affluence or poverty, you have choices to make that will determine your greatness or your folly. But it's always, always up to you. That's a good lesson to remember. I am determined to live it and to pass it on to my children, whenever I have some.

Our family surrounds us in this business. My husband, Warryn, produces us. Tina's husband, Teddy, plays drums for us sometimes. My sister, Thomasina, sings background vocals for us. And as I mentioned, my sister-in-law, Joi Campbell, is our stylist. It really is a family affair! In one way it's rewarding to be able to work with my relatives. On the flip side, if Mary Mary goes bust, then we feel responsible, but it's still important! Still, it's important to have people in this business who you know have your best interest at heart. They help to keep you grounded, by putting you in check when you get out of pocket. Sometimes we squabble, but like I said before, our fights always end in laughter.

The family members who aren't directly involved with our business give us tons of love and support, which is so important in this profession. I mentioned earlier that Tina and I grew up singing solos in the choir. So we've always been professional singers in our family's eyes. To them we are already super duper rock stars! One time I was in Ohio with my husband's family. We were on the elevator when a lady got in. This woman didn't know me from Adam and I didn't expect her to. But my little cousin, who was with me at the time, was so devastated and offended. When the woman got off the elevator, my cousin gasped, "Why she didn't even recognize you!" I told her that not everybody knows who I am. To which she responded, "Yes they do! Everybody in the world knows Mary Mary!" And she meant it, too! Her sincerity touched my heart and my funny bone. I tell you, you can't buy support and love like that! I love my family! They are the bomb!

I know God has truly blessed our family. I am humbled as I see how it's growing and prospering. To think it started with two young people who fell in love and decided to marry and have some kids, nine of them to be exact. I look to God to continue to protect and nurture us all. Tina and I look forward to a long, rewarding life with our spouses, surrounded by our children and loved ones.

FOOD FOR THOUGHT

1. Who are the people in your life who you can count on the most?

_____

_____

_____

_____

_____

_____

_____

_____

_____

_____

_____

_____

_____

_____

_____

_____

_____

_____

_____

_____

_____

2. In what ways do these people offer you support?

_____

_____

_____

_____

_____

_____

_____

_____

_____

_____

_____

_____

_____

3. How do you show your love and support for them?

_____

_____

_____

_____

_____

_____

_____

_____

_____

_____

_____

_____

_____

_____

_____

_____

_____

_____

_____

_____

_____

_____

_____

_____

_____

_____

_____

_____

_____

4. Do this: Tell the people who support you "thank you" for being there for you. If no one comes to mind, ask God to give you a "family" you can count on.

The Future

CHAPTER SIX

performing

backstage

rollin to the venue

Tina

Mary Mary's goal is to spread God's message as far and as fast as we can, to as many people as we can. We want to write music that will affect the world, not just now, but for generations to come. We don't just want to entertain people; we hope to change lives. In five years, I want to still be on good terms with all the behind-the-scenes people – management, executives, all the people who work around us, but who don't get the attention. I want them to be able to say good things about us, and that they'd love to work with us again and again. Of course we want to have sold millions of records, that would mean that we're reaching tons of people. In ten years, I hope we will have doubled or tripled our all that we will have accomplished in five years.

Erica

In the future, I have several things that I'd like to accomplish. I hope to write children's books. I have characters that are extensions of our "Little Girl" song. I want to teach children about self-esteem and having confidence in their abilities. I'd definitely like to try my hand at acting. I know that's something that both Tina and I are interested in. I'm open to television, film or whatever door God opens up. I'd also like to hone my craft, by developing my voice further. I would love to learn to sing other types of music and in so doing, discover and master every dynamic of my voice.

As a wife I want to be in love and stay married forever. I want to continue to learn everything I can about my husband and to grow together. I want to continue to be his friend, lover and whatever else he wants me to be and to get that in return.

Tina and I are so blessed. We sincerely desire to do our best for the Lord and to grow in our relationship with him. We look forward to meeting him face to face. We just want to take as many people along for the ride as we can!

FOOD FOR THOUGHT

Read Matthew 25: 1-46 and Luke 19: 12-27

1. What do these parables mean to you?

_____

_____

_____

_____

_____

_____

_____

_____

_____

_____

2. Based on the parables, what does God expect us to do with the gifts and opportunities he gives to us?

_____

_____

_____

_____

_____

_____

_____

_____

_____

_____

_____

_____

_____

_____

_____

_____

_____

_____

_____

_____

_____

3. Which one of the workers in the parables is most like you? Why?

_____

_____

_____

_____

_____

_____

_____

_____

_____

_____

_____

_____

_____

_____

_____

_____

_____

_____

_____

_____

_____

4. Pray this: "Heavenly Father, thank you for my chance at life. Help me to recognize and to make full use of all of the opportunities you give me."

Acknowledgements

TRUEink would like to thank the following individuals for their contribution to this project, listed below in no particular order.....

Encye - Kevin Jackson, China Flowers and Chaka Wilson
Kenneth Cole - Gidget Granillo
Meoshe - Broadway
Nike, Inc - Tim Bergevin, Jerry Sawyer and Adrian Miles
Chaudry - Bob Ditchik
Donahue Tuitt
Daven Baptiste
Marc Gerald
Nick Bolton
Kenneth Creer
Jeff Stern
Ingrid Hicks

Designskilz would like to thank
Paint Artist Management
Loco Motion Rental, Santa Monica
Ken Chernus/Studio 9351, Culver City
Richard's Photo Lab
Samy's Camera
Hasselblad
Edited by Emily Polsby, Doris Johnson
A special thanks to Erica and Tina Campbell of Mary Mary for being
TRANSPARENT

SINCERELY,
Mykel Mitchell   Sheeri Mitchell
Editor and Chief/   President TRUEink
Publisher TRUEink

Team Transparent Includes:
Design and Art Direction: designskilz advertising
Mary Mary as photgraphed by
d'lamar baptiste/daven@live4christ.com
Hair - China   *Make Up* - Jamalee
Assistant - Lauren Washington
Stylist - Derrick Wade for dlw and associates

Please visit us at **www.true-ink.com** *for downloads and more*

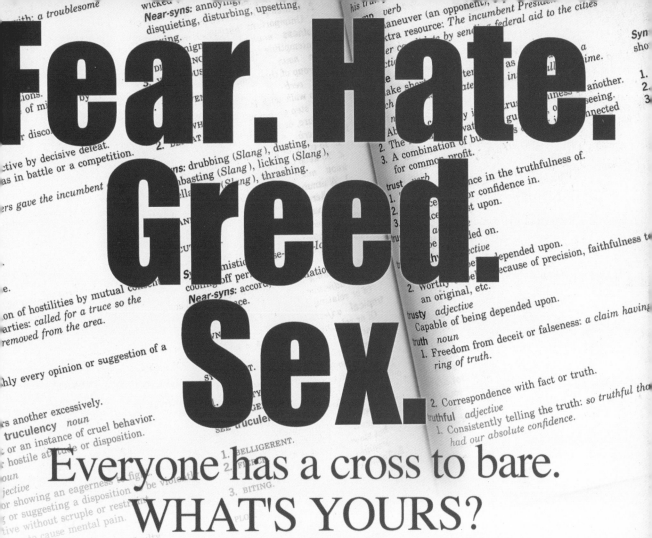